COMMUNIST CONTINUITY AND THE FIGHT FOR WOMEN'S LIBERATION

Part 1

Women's Liberation and the Line of March of the Working Class

PATHFINDER
New York London Montreal Sydney

Contents

Introduction   3
by Mary-Alice Waters, July 26, 1992

1. **The capitalist ideological offensive against women today**   8
   Excerpt from introduction to Cosmetics, Fashions, and the Exploitation of Women
   by Mary-Alice Waters, November 1985

2. **The struggle by women against their oppression as a sex is a form of the class struggle**   17
   Report adopted by the National Convention of the Socialist Workers Party, August 7, 1979
   by Mary-Alice Waters
   > *Reprinted from* International Internal Discussion Bulletin, *vol. XVI, no. 6, October 1979*

3. **Socialist revolution and the struggle for women's liberation**   37
   Resolution adopted by the National Convention of the Socialist Workers Party, August 7, 1979
   > *Reprinted from* 1979 World Congress of the Fourth International:
   > Major resolutions and reports, *special supplement to* Intercontinental Press

4. **Social weight and revolutionary strategy for the transformation of the labor movement**   83
   Excerpt from report adopted by SWP National Committee, April 29, 1979
   by Jack Barnes
   > *From 'A new stage of revolutionary working-class politics,'*
   > *from Part II: 'The roots of revolutionary strategy.' Reprinted from*
   > The Changing Face of U.S. Politics: The Proletarian Party and the Trade Unions

5. **Affirmative action gains for women in industry and the way forward for the women's movement**   87
   Excerpt from report adopted by SWP National Committee, April 29, 1979
   by Jack Barnes
   > *From 'A new stage of revolutionary working-class politics,'*
   > *from Part III: 'Resolving the crisis of proletarian leadership.' Reprinted from*
   > The Changing Face of U.S. Politics: The Proletarian Party and the Trade Unions

INTRODUCTION
by Mary-Alice Waters

From Wichita to Buffalo, from Boston to Milwaukee, from New Orleans to New York, a new generation of women is taking to the streets to defend women's rights. A new fighting layer of the working class is learning to see the defense of these rights as inseparable from defending the democratic rights of all and the class interests of workers.

As thousands of women come to recognize the need to *act* to prevent hard-fought gains from being lost, they are rejecting the myth that the oppression of women as a sex was vanquished by the "second wave" of the feminist movement in the early 1970s. They are confronting all the fundamental questions that previous generations of women fighting for their liberation have addressed, and that the working-class vanguard must answer if it is to advance toward socialism.

Why are women oppressed? How did that oppression begin? Why are opponents of a woman's right to choose and of the Equal Rights Amendment so determined to perpetuate laws and customs that deny women an equal role in society? Who benefits? What social forces have the power to end the second-class status of women, and have common interests in the fight for women's liberation?

These three Education for Socialists bulletins—which bear the common title *Communist Continuity and the Fight for Women's Liberation: Documents of the Socialist Workers Party, 1971–86*—aim to make available raw materials that will help the generation of women and men now joining battle in defense of women's rights find the answers to these and similar questions and win them to the communist movement.

The bulletins should be read as a "work in progress." They draw together in one place some of the most important resolutions, reports, and articles that come out of the active involvement of the Socialist Workers Party and Young Socialist Alliance in the fight for women's rights since a new feminist movement arose at the end of the 1960s. A product of the deep-going economic and social changes that began with Washington's preparations for entry into World War II, the "second wave" of feminism was one of the powerful components of the radicalization of the 1960s and 1970s that profoundly affected the working class and changed political consciousness on an even broader scale.

Part I of the series, *Women's Liberation and the Line of March of the Working Class,* contains the main programmatic documents, or articles and reports based on them, that have been adopted by the Socialist Workers Party since 1979. Central to this bulletin is the resolution "Socialist revolution and the struggle for women's liberation," adopted by the SWP convention in August 1979. The resolution in its final form was the product of collective discussion and debate in the international movement the SWP was part of at that time, the Fourth International, and is enriched by the varied experiences in many countries it incorporates. The initial drafting of the resolution, however, as well as the final editing, was done by the leadership of the SWP. While one or two points would be developed differently if written today, and others added, the resolution remains the best guide we have on the central place and weight of the fight for women's liberation in the strategic line of march of the working class toward socialism.

Other materials in Part I develop specific points that are incorporated in the international resolution. The excerpts from other reports often explain at greater length or more clearly how we arrived at some of the conclusions that are codified in the resolution.

"The capitalist ideological offensive against women today" builds on the international resolution to take up a number of important questions that came to the fore in the early 1980s. It is excerpted from the introduction to the book *Cosmetics, Fashions, and the Exploitation of Women*; that introduction was based on a report adopted by the SWP National Committee entitled "Confronting the leadership pressures on women during a retreat of the labor movement," which is contained in Part II of this series.

All of the material in Part I registers the political conquests of the SWP since the late 1970s, as the party cadres deepened their orientation toward the industrial working class and unions, building a party that is proletarian not only in its program and perspectives but overwhelmingly in its composition, political milieu, and rhythms of activity as well. As part of that process, deepening our understanding of the character and central importance of the fight to end women's oppression as a sex was indispensable.

Reading this material together with the SWP resolutions and reports contained in *The Changing Face of U.S. Politics: The Proletarian Party and the Trade Unions*, published by Pathfinder Press, will place it in an even broader national and international class framework. The women involved in the work documented in these bulletins were the same women who were advancing the fights in their plants and unions and in the broader working-class movement. And they were changing themselves and their party in the process.

The documents in Part II, *Women, Leadership, and Proletarian Norms of the Communist Movement*, register the party's political progress as we conquered the kinds of working-class attitudes and norms of functioning that make it possible for workers, members of oppressed nationalities, and women to develop as party leaders. The ability of the Socialist Workers Party cadres to discuss objectively and lead politically on the range of questions documented here has been unique in the communist movement. These questions include:

- the need for affirmative action within the party;
- why quotas, exclusive caucuses, and exclusionary social activities are destructive to comradely relations and leadership development in a revolutionary centralist working-class organization;
- eradicating the cancer of race-baiting;
- establishing that violence of any kind against women destroys party democracy and political equality and is incompatible with membership;
- helping members with children maximize their political activity, without pretending the party can or should take responsibility for child care.

The SWP has conquered these proletarian norms and rejected the petty-bourgeois attitudes and functioning prevalent in other organizations that pretend to speak in the interests of the working class. Had we not been able to do so, the SWP too would have been torn apart in petty factional battles and clique fights similar to those that have decimated the Communist Party, among others, in recent years.

Part III of the series is entitled *Abortion Rights, the ERA, and the Rebirth of a Feminist Movement: The Party Campaigns for Women's Rights*. It contains the resolution adopted by the SWP in 1971, the first party convention after the mass movement for women's liberation burst on the political scene; it registers the party's enthusiastic support for, and involvement in, that revolutionary development. While this might seem unremarkable today, at the time it set the SWP apart from virtually all other working-class organizations.

Part III also contains "Feminism and the Marxist movement," which took up and answered the challenge of the "socialist-feminist" currents that emerged as part of the new radicalization. These currents decried the supposed theoretical inadequacies of Marxism and argued the need for a new theoretical framework to chart a course toward women's liberation.

The core of Part III, however, documents the work of the Socialist Workers Party and Young Socialist Alliance to build the abortion rights movement in the early 1970s and, a few years later, to mobilize the kind of movement that would have been necessary to win the Equal Rights Amendment to the U.S. Constitution. These reports and articles draw together the work we were part of and capture the campaigning, interventionist spirit of the party and youth; they provide the best guide for today, as we respond to the new struggles that are unfolding.

As we collectively read, study, discuss, and use this material, we will gain a better appreciation of what is most valuable in preparing us to participate in today's struggles. We will also better understand the accomplishments and conquests of the battles that have brought us this far.

In bringing these documents together, no attempt has been made to edit them in light of later experience or to change formulations or points in early documents that are clarified and explained more accurately in later materials. Readers will be able to see for themselves the evolution of the party's collective thinking and growing political comprehension of a range of questions.

JULY 26, 1992

Contents of Part II

Part II—Women, leadership, and proletarian norms of the communist movement

1. **Confronting the leadership pressures on women during a retreat of the labor movement**
   Report on 'Preparing the election of the National Committee,' adopted by SWP National Committee, May 1985
   by Mary-Alice Waters
   Reprinted from Information Bulletin *no. 2 in 1985, June 1985*

2. **Forging the leadership of a proletarian party**
   Excerpt from report adopted by SWP National Committee, May 1979
   by Mary-Alice Waters
   Reprinted from SWP Discussion Bulletin, *vol. 36, no. 13, July 1979*

3. **Leading the party into industry**
   Excerpt from report adopted by SWP National Committee, February 1978
   by Jack Barnes
   Reprinted from Party Organizer, *vol. 2, no. 2, April 1978*

4. **Violence against women is incompatible with party membership**
   Excerpt from 'Political Committee report on Control Commission recommendations,' report adopted by SWP National Convention, August 13, 1977
   by Linda Jenness
   Reprinted from Internal Information Bulletin *no. 7 in 1977, September 1977*

5. **Communist norms and nonexclusive social affairs**
   Report adopted by SWP National Convention, August 13, 1977
   by Catarino Garza
   Reprinted from Internal Information Bulletin *no. 7 in 1977, September 1977*

6. **Race-baiting and communist leadership**
   Report adopted by SWP National Committee, February 1986
   by Mac Warren
   Reprinted from Information Bulletin *no. 1 in 1986, April 1986*

7. **Children, child care, and membership norms of a proletarian party**
   Report adopted by SWP Political Committee, June 18, 1986
   by Jack Barnes
   Reprinted from Information Bulletin *no. 2 in 1986, August 1986*

   ### Appendix 1:
   Letter to Political Committee from James, June 12, 1986
   Letter to Political Committee from Vivian, June 6, 1986
   Reprinted from Information Bulletin *no. 2 in 1986, August 1986*

   ### Appendix 2:
   Excerpt from report on women's liberation movement
   From report adopted by SWP National Committee, March 14, 1971
   by Betsey Stone
   Reprinted from Internal Information Bulletin *no. 2 in 1971, April 1971*

Contents of part III

Part III—Abortion rights, the ERA, and the rebirth of a feminist movement: The party campaigns for women's rights

1. The abortion struggle: What have we accomplished, where should we go from here?
   by Betsey Stone and Mary-Alice Waters
   Reprinted from SWP Discussion Bulletin, *vol. 31, no. 19, July 1973*

2. Feminism and the Marxist movement
   by Mary-Alice Waters
   Reprinted from Pathfinder pamphlet; originally published in October 1972 International Socialist Review

3. Toward a mass feminist movement
   Resolution adopted by SWP National Convention, August 1971
   Reprinted from SWP Discussion Bulletin, *vol. 29, no. 4, April 1971*

4. Emergence of a new feminist movement
   Excerpt from 'Perspectives and Lessons of the New Radicalization,' political resolution adopted by the SWP National Convention, August 1971
   Reprinted from A Revolutionary Strategy for the 70s: Documents of the Socialist Workers Party

5. Struggles by women reflect the depth of the social crisis and radicalization
   Excerpts from 'Prospects for Socialism in America,' political resolution adopted by SWP National Convention, August 1975
   Reprinted from The Changing Face of U.S. Politics: The Proletarian Party and the Trade Unions
   From Part IV: 'Changing Character and Composition of the Working Class'
   From Part V: 'Radicalization and Mobilization of the Allies of the Proletariat'

6. The fight for an independent women's movement
   Report adopted by SWP National Committee, February 25, 1978, by Willie Mae Reid
   Reprinted from Party Organizer, *vol. 2, no. 3, May 1978*

   Appendix: April 1977 National NOW Conference
   2,000 feminists debate strategy for movement, by Nancy Cole
   Reprinted from the Militant, *May 6, 1977*

   SWP answers red-baiting, by Mary-Alice Waters
   Reprinted from the Militant, *May 6, 1977*

7. Campaigning for the ERA

   (a) Impact of July 9, 1978, 100,000-strong march on Washington for the ERA and the perspectives for NOW
   Report adopted by SWP Political Bureau, November 3, 1978, by Wendy Lyons
   Reprinted from Party Organizer, *vol. 2, no. 8, November 1978*

   (b) Labor for Equal Rights Now (LERN) and the Illinois ERA campaign
   Report adopted by SWP national steelworkers fraction, February 24, 1980, by Pat Grogan
   Reprinted from Party Organizer, *vol. 4, no. 1, April 1980*

   (c) Mortal blow to the ERA: NOW leadership capitulates to Washington's third militarization drive
   Excerpt from report on 'Imperialist Militarization and the Draft,' adopted by SWP National Committee, May 25, 1980, by Andrea Morell
   Reprinted from Party Organizer, *vol. 5, no. 2 April 1981*

THE CAPITALIST IDEOLOGICAL OFFENSIVE AGAINST WOMEN TODAY
Excerpt from introduction to 'Cosmetics, Fashions, and the Exploitation of Women'
by Mary-Alice Waters

Post–World War II reaction

At the end of World War II, the U.S. rulers came out on top of the imperialist heap, with their main capitalist rivals devastated. The postwar workers' upsurge in Western Europe was crushed. The 1945–46 strike wave in the United States ended in a stalemate. These factors established the preconditions for a quarter century of capitalist economic expansion during which broad layers of U.S. working people were able to wrest significant concessions from the bosses.

At the same time, however, the world system of imperialist domination had been weakened. While the imperial masters were fighting each other, the masses of colonial slaves rebelled. Revolutionary struggles for independence exploded throughout Asia and Africa. Despite enormous losses and devastation, the Soviet Union emerged victorious over German imperialism. The workers and peasants of Eastern Europe and China put an end to landlord-capitalist rule in vast new areas of the globe.

The response of the imperialist powers to these mortal blows was to launch and then expand the cold war against the Soviet Union and its new allies. The imperialists attempted to militarily crush the national liberation forces in Korea and Vietnam. Some individuals at top levels of the U.S. government gave serious consideration to using nuclear weapons against the people of those two countries and thus to repeating the horrors inflicted on the civilian populations of Hiroshima and Nagasaki a few years earlier.

In the United States, the domestic side of the cold war was an anticommunist witch-hunt. It was aimed at destroying the unity and combativity of the industrial unions born in the great labor upsurge of the 1930s. It sought to turn back the postwar surge in the fight for Black civil rights. It was intended to sow fear, division, and demoralization among all those fighting for social progress. Through the witch-hunt, the employers sought to assure the conditions of labor "peace" and political passivity necessary for an extended period of intensified exploitation of working people and accelerated capitalist accumulation.

The witch-hunt was at its peak as the 1950s began to unfold. The depoliticization of working-class fighters in the unions deepened. There was less and less motion in the labor movement around social questions and no extensive political life independent of the employers' parties. As a result of these conditions, the membership of the Socialist Workers Party—as well as that of the Communist Party and other organizations on the left—declined sharply and rapidly. Socialists became more and more isolated politically. The SWP was forced into a largely semisectarian existence; its activity could no longer be based on an organized political life as part of a working-class vanguard within the industrial unions.

That was the political context in which the debate over cosmetics, fashions, and the exploitation of women broke out in the SWP. It registered the impact of the U.S. rulers' political offensive to divide workers and weaken their class consciousness.

During World War II women had been incorporated into the labor force in larger numbers than ever before. Even more importantly, they were hired to perform many jobs from which women had previously been excluded. This broadened the social and political horizons of tens of millions of women who had formerly been trapped in the stultifying confines of the home or employed only in jobs traditionally hiring female labor. This also brought irreversible changes in the way that both women and men thought about women's place in society. When the war was over, there were millions of women and men who wanted to maintain these newly conquered social and economic relations.

For the employing class, however, increasing economic independence and social equality for women is incompatible with intensified superexploitation of female labor power. Hence, the deliberate promotion during postwar years of the "feminine mystique," as it later came to be known. This extensive political and ideological campaign was aimed at rolling back the changes in attitudes about women's proper role. It was promoted in order to reinforce the idea that women—whether or not they are part of the labor force—should first and foremost be wives, mothers, and housekeepers. Thus women should accept employment at lower wages and under worse conditions. Women should spend less time on union activity or political concerns and should take less interest in them.

Women were not the only target of the rulers' ideological campaign. This reactionary assault, waged through the mass media, schools, and churches, was directed toward reversing the attitudes of both sexes concerning women's social role. But its impact on women was different. To a large extent women, like other oppressed layers of capitalist society, internalize the pressures on them. They place limitations on themselves, often unconsciously. They accept the socially prescribed roles, and, in fact, often promote the conditions that perpetuate their own oppression.

Through the "cosmetics" debate that took place among members of the Socialist Workers Party, we get a glimpse of the diverse, if not so subtle, ways in which the postwar period of reaction affected even women and men who were socialists and conscious champions of women's liberation. We see how the pressures affected the way people thought about themselves.

Changes in women's social conditions since 1950

Since the early 1950s, of course, there have been extensive changes in the economic and social conditions facing women in the United States. The domestic and international political situation has been vastly altered, as well.

Most importantly, the accelerated expansion of capitalism in the postwar years brought with it an even greater incorporation of women into the labor market than during World War II. In 1950, 33.9 percent of women sixteen years of age and over were in the labor force. By 1960 that figure had risen to 37.7 percent. In 1970 it was 43.3 percent. And by 1983, more than half of all working-age women—52.9 percent—were in the labor force. During that thirty-three-year period, the percentage increase of women who were in the labor market was slightly more than the percentage increase during the seventy years between 1890 and 1960!

Women today account for 43 percent of the labor force, as compared with 29 percent in 1950. This marks a qualitative advance in the economic independence of women and consequently a change in their social status.

It is also important, however, to take a look at the changes in *where* women are employed. Two of the most carefully promoted myths are the notions that working women have generally "escaped" from industrial jobs, and that this represents a rising economic and social status for women. The reality is far more complex. The most important advances for women—although directly involving only a small percentage of women—have been precisely those that have integrated them more deeply into the most strongly organized, predominantly male, sectors of the industrial working class.

The expansion of the labor market in general since 1950 has been marked by an increase in clerical, commercial, and other nonindustrial jobs relative to those in industrial production. Since the influx of women into the labor market has been much more rapid than that of men, the percentage of employed women working industrial jobs has declined.

Over this same thirty-five-year period, however, there has also been a much greater incorporation of women into industrial production. *In fact, the percentage of industrial workers who are women has significantly risen since World War II.* Moreover, since the early 1970s women have fought their way into many types of jobs from which they had previously been excluded. The categories used by government statistical bureaus make it difficult to obtain fully reliable figures, but the trend is nonetheless clear.

For example, while the total number of men

categorized as "blue-collar workers" increased by 29 percent between 1950 and 1981, the number of women in such jobs went up by some 61.5 percent; this increased the percentage of workers who are women in such job categories from 15.4 percent to 18.6 percent over that thirty-one-year period.

The increase is even more noticeable in the subcategories of "operatives" (assemblers, punch- and stamping-press operators, welders, sewing-machine operators, truck drivers, fork-lift operators, etc.) and "craft" workers (carpenters, electricians, sheet-metal workers, tool-and-die makers, mechanics, etc.).

In craft positions, the gains for women are especially striking, since they had been largely frozen out of these jobs until recently. The number of men holding such jobs went up by 58.5 percent between 1950 and 1981; the number of women leaped by 327 percent. The percentage of women in the crafts is still small, but it has grown from 2.5 percent in 1950 to 6.3 percent in 1981.

Among operatives, the number of men went up by 8 percent between 1950 and 1981, while the number of women grew by 35 percent; this increased the proportion of women in such production jobs from 27.4 percent to 32.3 percent.

The number of women mine workers grew from 0.7 percent of miners in 1972 to 2.2 percent in 1981. Among underground miners, the percentage of women hired went from almost zero in 1973–74 to between 8 and 10 percent in the first five years of the 1980s.[1] [Notes are on page 16.]

Women in the industrial unions

If we look at the position of women as part of the organized labor movement, a similarly complex picture emerges.

The level of unionization of women workers has declined over the past several decades as part of the overall sharp decline in union membership. This fact tells only part of the story, however.

The gains for women in industrial production jobs previously off-limits to them—whether in mining, steel, auto, or whatever—have usually meant integration into the industrial unions in a qualitatively new way. Probably the best example is the employment of women in coal mining and the growing role of women in the United Mine Workers union. Women have been fighting their way into jobs such as coal mining. This is precisely because unions such as the UMWA have won contracts that guarantee higher average wages and better benefits than women can find in traditional "female" occupations. Moreover, women are guaranteed wages and conditions equal to male co-workers in the same job categories. Women who have busted into these industries are often among the most conscious unionists. Many have learned through their own experiences why class solidarity and organization are so indispensable. They know that without union protection they would not stand a chance against the bosses' attempts to divide the work force and turn other workers against them.

Women in the industrial unions, of course, still have to fight discrimination, prejudice, sexual harassment on the job, and "reclassification" schemes to downgrade their wages and conditions and those of other, more recently hired workers. Women often have to help their union brothers learn that sex discrimination weakens the entire labor movement.

But it is precisely by fighting their way into such jobs that women can have an impact on the social conditions that keep the value of their labor power substantially lower than that of men. It is in such industrial union jobs that women are in the best position to develop mutual respect and confidence with male co-workers, gain self-confidence and class consciousness, and affect the attitudes of both men and women about women's role in society.

A woman who works on an assembly line has a different relationship to the men around her than a woman who works as a secretary. And both are in a qualitatively different economic and social situation vis-à-vis men than a woman who remains outside the labor market altogether.

Thus, the changes in the employment statistics for women over the last thirty-five years, and the changes in where women work, codify *social* advances affecting tens of millions of women and men.

Other changes important to women's social position also occurred during the postwar period. For the first time ever, advances in medical science gave women access to birth control methods that were relatively safe and certain, and that were under their own control.

Educational levels rose in general, and women won broader access to job training programs and higher education.

Increasing labor productivity and capitalism's competitive expansion into new sectors of commodity production and distribution created a mass market in the imperialist countries for household appliances and prepared foods. While women have hardly escaped from their domestic slavery, their work load has been eased. A wide range of such commodities have now become incorporated into the historically determined—and changing—value of labor power, to that extent raising the living standards of workers and their families.

An insoluble contradiction

Since the beginning of the industrial revolution in the eighteenth century, capitalist expansion and the lash of competition have dictated the incorporation of larger and larger numbers of women into the labor force. This is so because capital always seeks to incorporate into the work force large numbers of workers in oppressed social categories (in this case women), the value of whose labor power under capitalism is less than that of others. This is a key way in which the employers drive down the overall average value of labor power by heightening competition among workers for jobs.

The development of capitalism, however, creates real—and ultimately insoluble—contradictions for the exploiting class. The capitalists' increasing purchase of women's capacities as wage laborers inevitably brings in its wake greater economic independence for women. It contributes to further disintegration of the family, and expands the need for the household appliances and prepared foods noted above. These factors, in turn, tend to raise the value of women's labor power, to raise the wages they can command in the labor market on average, other things being equal.[2]

Through their experiences in the work force and the unions, women in growing numbers also begin to think in broader social terms and to act as political beings. They become increasingly class conscious. They play an expanding role in struggles by the labor movement that can wrest higher wages from the employers and social programs from the capitalist government, thus pushing up the value of labor power for the entire working class.

These were the kinds of economic and social developments that took place in the decades of the post–World War II capitalist expansion, weakening the foundations on which the entire edifice of women's oppression is built. As these objective preconditions combined with the political changes of the 1950s and 1960s—above all, the civil rights and anti–Vietnam War movements—the "second wave" of feminism exploded onto the scene. As a result of the women's liberation struggles since the end of the 1960s, further broad advances have taken place in women's attitudes toward themselves and their place in society, as well as in the views of men on these matters.

Rulers' reaction against gains by women

The period of accelerated post–World War II capitalist expansion came to an end in the mid-1970s. As this took place, the shifts in the economic and social conditions of women, and the changing attitudes and expectations accompanying them, increasingly clashed with the economic interests—that is, the profits—of the U.S. ruling class. This conflict lies beneath the political and ideological campaign directed against women's rights that we are now living through, just as a similar conflict led to the reactionary promotion of the "feminine mystique" in the late 1940s and 1950s.

Today the employers are once again making a concerted political effort to roll back, or at least slow down, some of the changes in consciousness about women's place in society. They are taking aim at concrete gains won through hard struggle in the 1960s and 1970s, such as abortion rights and affirmative action programs.

The goal of the bosses and their government is not to drive women out of the labor force, but to undermine their class consciousness and political self-confidence. The goal is to make women more willing to acquiesce in attacks on wages, working conditions, social services, affirmative action programs, and equality on the job. In this way, the employers are attempting to hold back the increase in the value of women's labor power (and thereby that of the class as a whole), and to enforce greater discipline and "productivity" by imposing speedup and more dangerous working conditions.

These attacks on women's rights are part of a broader offensive that the U.S. capitalist class has been waging for more than a decade. The target is all working people, and all those whose race, sex, language, or national origin is used by the ruling class to single them out for superexploitation and special oppression. The employers are determined to fundamentally shift the relationship of forces between capital and labor that was established following the post–World War II strike wave.

This intensifying capitalist offensive began with the 1974–75 world recession and picked up steam with the 1980–82 recession. It is directed against the wages, job conditions, democratic rights, and organizations of the working class. It is aimed at heading off progress toward political independence by the working class—toward any notion that labor should develop and fight for its own positions on social and political questions, independent of and opposed to those of the bosses and bosses' parties.

This offensive has been registered in a rightward shift of the entire bipartisan structure of capitalist politics in the United States. It has been accompanied by a sustained ideological offensive aimed at dividing the working class more deeply between employed and unemployed, and along the lines of race, sex, age, "skill levels," language, and national origin. A special goal has been to reverse gains won by Blacks and women, who over the previous period fought their way through some of the barriers that keep them confined to second-class status in capitalist society in general, and within the labor force in particular.

Parallel to this domestic offensive has been an escalation of U.S. aggression abroad, especially in Central America and the Caribbean. As part of the preparations for war, there has been an enormous increase in U.S. military spending. We have seen a constant barrage of anticommunist propaganda, directed above all against Nicaragua, Cuba, and the Salvadoran freedom fighters, but also against Angola, Vietnam, the South African and Palestinian peoples. This has been accompanied by a domestic spy hunt and antiunion "industrial security" campaign. Through the concerted political drive on all these fronts, Wall Street and Washington are trying to bludgeon and con the U.S. working class into believing that *their* foreign policy is in *our* interests.

One result of this sustained economic and political offensive, with all its reactionary ideological offshoots, has been a deepening class polarization in the United States. Not everyone is suffering from the policies that the employers are putting into effect. To the contrary, tens of millions of individuals in middle-class and professional layers are *benefiting* from these policies. Some layers of the working class have also improved their situation—even if the insecurities and pressures that are common to their class also bear down on them. To varying degrees, all these social layers are being pulled to the right politically.

On the other hand, the big majority of workers and working farmers are taking stiffer and stiffer blows. The bosses' offensive has run into resistance, however. There has been opposition to two-tier wage scales, bank foreclosures on struggling farmers, and U.S. military intervention in Central America. Working people have mobilized in defense of Black rights. Struggles have been fought around women's rights and immigrants' rights.

All of these are labor issues—issues on which the labor movement must have its own policies and defend its own class interests and those of its allies. All are questions on which there is reflection, concern, and a growing willingness to take action on the part of workers. Broad and growing sectors of working people—on the farms and in the factories—are becoming aware that there are interconnections among these many battlefronts.

So far, defeats and setbacks for working people continue to outnumber victories, and the bosses and their politicians retain the initiative. But that has not put a stop to resistance. To the contrary, the willingness and desire of working people to fight back continues to assert itself.

The class polarization and the experiences that are generating it give an impulse to the politicization and radicalization of the most combative workers. But these same developments also embolden rightist proponents of national-chauvinist, racist, anti-Semitic, antiwoman, and antiunion prejudices, as well as other reactionary ideas.

This is the political context in which we need to place the current attacks on women's rights by the employers and their government.

Bosses reinforce antiwoman prejudices

When the bosses go on a stepped-up offensive to shift the relationship of forces in their favor, they play every card in the deck—war and the threat of military aggression abroad; more naked use of the cops and courts at home (whether against Blacks, immigrant workers, farmers, or strikers); massive cuts in social services; tax hikes; union busting and concession contracts. At the same time, they wage a political campaign to justify their course as being in the interests of "all of us." They talk about "equality of sacrifice," the "national interest," "labor-management cooperation," and "common cultural values."

Within this framework, the rulers single out special targets as part of their broad frontal assault. One of these is always the progressive changes taking place in women's social status. The employers are aiming at the advances of working-class women especially, but the barrage is necessarily directed against all women. The second sex must be taught to know its place.

The attack on women's rights is fundamental to the success of the capitalist offensive. Discrimination against women is one of the most important ways in which the rulers work to deepen divisions within the working class. Its acceptance helps the bosses keep the labor movement shackled to a narrow trade union perspective, instead of thinking in broader social terms and acting politically to advance the interests of the oppressed and exploited. The perpetuation of women's subordinate status is one more obstacle along the road to independent working-class political action.

The employers aim to undermine working-class women's consciousness of themselves *as workers, as part of the working class,* and instead to heighten their consciousness of themselves as women—not in the feminist sense, but in all the retrograde ways that are drummed into women from childhood. The employing class seeks to reinforce the prejudices about women's proper place and domestic role. It seeks to convince women that they *want* to be dependent on a man, with the second-class status that entails.

Such prejudices, and the ways women internalize them, go back millennia. But the rise and development of capitalism progressively undermines them, as it forces women out of the home and off the farm and pushes them as individuals into the labor market—with all the brutality inherent in the capitalist mode of production.

The capitalists' offensive against women's rights is not aimed at driving women out of the work force. That is historically precluded. The percentage of wage and salaried workers who are female has been rising, from one plateau to another, ever since the beginning of the industrial revolution. Instead, the aim is to make women more vulnerable to increased exploitation. The goal is not to push women *out* of the labor market but to push them *down*—to jobs with fewer paid holidays, more piece work, less safety, shorter lunch breaks, less union protection, and lower wages.

Women have always made up an important component of the pool of unemployed workers that Marx called the industrial reserve army of labor. This reserve army never disappears under capitalism, even in the best of times. But in a period of capitalist stagnation such as we have lived through over the last decade, the owners of capital need to expand this army of the unemployed in order to intensify competition among workers and thus drive down wages. Hundreds of thousands of women workers were forced into its ranks during the 1980–82 recession, eroding some of the employment gains they had previously won.

The bosses' ideological campaign seeks to reinforce the idea among both sexes that women are "natural" recruits to this reserve army. They are "normally" only marginal workers, temporary workers, part-time workers, home workers. Women are only a "second" wage earner in the family. In periods of rising joblessness, there are always assertions by ruling-class "opinion molders" that unemployment statistics are artificially high, since women should not really be counted as unemployed in the same way as men, who are considered the main breadwinners. This propaganda is aimed at convincing women to accept, with less resistance and resentment, temporary unemployment, or new jobs at lower wages. All this is true despite the increase in female heads of household, a trend that will continue as the evolution of capitalism continues to disintegrate the family.

The capitalists want women to blame themselves, not the social relations of production, for the economic and social problems they confront every day. The goal is to make women feel guilty that their children are being permanently damaged by "abandonment" in child-care facilities (if they exist), or are being turned into lonely latchkey delinquents. Rather than demanding—as a *right*—both child-care facilities and equal access to high-paying jobs previously barred to them, women are pushed toward being grateful for any job, at any wage.

Part of the rulers' strategy is also to deepen race divisions. They seek to break down solidarity and intensify competition between women workers who are fighting their way into nontraditional jobs and Black workers, who constitute a large proportion of the politically more conscious, vanguard layers of the working class. Since women are getting jobs that men "ought" to have, they are alleged to be responsible for the high rate of unemployment of Black males. The employers also attempt to pit white women and Black women against each other along similar lines.

Even the notion that backward, prejudiced men are the source of women's problems is accorded a favored niche in the employers' propaganda arsenal as an alternative to the truth that the capitalist system is responsible for perpetuating the oppression of women.

Because the advances in women's status in the 1960s and 1970s were so broad, and the changes in consciousness so sweeping, the counteroffensive against women's rights in the last few years has been all the more concerted. It has taken numerous forms:

- The defeat of the Equal Rights Amendment.
- The onslaught against abortion rights—from the withholding of government funds; to the bombing of clinics; to the propaganda, day in and day out, that abortion is murder, murder, murder. State, local, and federal legislation and court rulings have placed more and more restrictions on abortion rights, and government officials are seeking to make even deeper inroads.
- The concerted drive to roll back affirmative action gains, to foster the "white-male" backlash against Blacks and women.
- Glorification of the family, built around the theme of a woman's special fulfillment of herself as a mother. Supermom is in. She often works a full-time job. That is accepted. But it's only when she comes home, we are told, that her real responsibilities, and her true possibilities for fulfillment, begin. Supermom makes sure her kids—and husband— don't suffer too much for her selfish absorption in her own life. And, deep down, she has a lot of doubts about whether she's doing the right thing. Isn't this "new woman" wonderful? How many guilt-tripping articles with that reactionary message have been published in the last few years?

Decline of the women's movement

The counteroffensive to roll back the gains women have made has been registered in a decline of the women's movement. Since 1977 the National Organization for Women (NOW) has been turned more and more into an electoralist appendage of the capitalist two-party system. The thousands of small circles of feminist activists that sprang up in the early 1970s have disappeared. The few groups that have survived concentrate largely on specific interests such as women's health clinics or art. Others have been drawn into reactionary campaigns demanding more cops as an answer to the continuing reality of rape, or calling for censorship laws as the way to deal with pornography.

The last time a sizable women's rights action occurred in the United States was 1978. That was the 100,000-strong July 9, 1978, march on Washington called by NOW to demand an extension of the deadline for ERA ratification. There has been no women's liberation action of similar size or impact since then. This is true despite the potential that existed for ongoing mass mobilizations around the ERA and the growing desire of women to act in defense of abortion rights.

That situation will not continue indefinitely. There is growing pressure for a change. There are already indications of a pickup in organized protests responding to the escalating attacks on women's right to abortion.

But the fact remains that there has been no mass, fighting women's movement in the streets or anywhere else for some years. The kind of mass-action movement from which women gain self-confidence as they fight to change things that vitally affect their lives; the kind of action movement through which women learn how to mobilize millions to fight for their rights—that kind of movement does not exist today. The women's liberation forces are on the defensive, not the offensive.

This situation is not unique to the United States. It is a phenomenon that, to varying degrees, marks virtually all capitalist countries where the women's liberation movement had a significant impact in the 1970s. The reasons for this decline are fundamentally the same everywhere. It is one of the fruits of the incapacity of the labor officialdom to mount an effective fight back against the capitalist austerity drive that began with the 1974–75 worldwide recession. Prospects for advancing the fight for women's liberation are not independent of the historic course of the working-class movement, even if women's rights battles can and do surge ahead on occasion—as they did in the early 1970s—and help show the way forward.

All the conservatizing pressures described above have been mounting for nearly a decade now. And they have borne down with a special weight on women. This is not an argument for pessimism about the future; to the contrary, there are some small signs of new struggles on the horizon. It is merely a statement of fact about the past ten years. Moreover, it explains a number of significant and well-documented phenomena that mirror the enforced social and political retreat of women: the sharp increase in childbearing among women in their thirties; the rise in teenage pregnancy rates; the flight by many liberals, including prominent feminists, from an active and outspoken defense of affirmative action quotas for women and Blacks.

Women in industry

Women who are full-time industrial workers and part of the organized labor movement are in the best position to resist the conservatizing pressures that all women are subjected to by the economic, political, and ideological offensive of the ruling class. The reason is simple. The fundamental line of division, of deepening cleavage, is *a class polarization.* Not all women—and not all women who work—are hit by the offensive with equal force and in the same ways. Not only the economic squeeze, but also the necessity to fight back weigh more heavily on working-class women. The reactionary ideological and political offensive of the employers has less fertile ground in which to take root in the working class in general than among middle-class layers.

Women who are industrial workers and union members have a degree of self-confidence that comes from knowing that they can sell their labor power and survive. They are not so economically dependent on a man, and this gives them a greater element of independence in making important decisions that affect their lives. Moreover, they have acquired at least the beginning of working-class consciousness through understanding that they have a better chance at improving wages and working conditions by joining together with fellow workers to defend themselves against the employer. Moreover, despite the bosses' attempts to foster animosities toward them by male workers, women in industry frequently work alongside men in job situations where each depends on the other and relations of mutual respect and confidence can develop.

While women who are industrial workers are less susceptible to right-wing demagogy and reactionary "solutions" to their problems, however, they are nonetheless not immune. They are constantly fighting the bosses' attempts to convince them and their male co-workers that they are not really workers; that being part of the labor force is only a passing moment in women's lives; that the really important thing for them is that they will leave the labor force to raise a family; or that, having already left the labor market to raise a family, they are now past their prime, and should be glad to find a boss "willing" to employ them.

This kind of reactionary propaganda—in a period of working-class political retreat—affects even the most politically conscious women and men. That is why it is helpful to look back at the 1950s and learn from history. It is useful to see how the reactionary offensive against women's rights in that period found an echo inside the Socialist Workers Party. It helps in understanding some of the pressures today, and arms us to deal with them more consciously.

NOTES

1. The above figures are from U.S. Bureau of the Census, *Statistical Abstract of the United States: 1985* (105th edition.) Washington D.C., 1984.

2. In the first volume of *Capital*, Karl Marx explained the factors that determine the value of workers' labor power in the following terms:

"The value of labour-power is determined, as in the case of every other commodity, by the labour-time necessary for the production, and consequently also the reproduction, of this specific article. In so far as it has value, it represents no more than a definite quantity of the average social labour objectified in it. Labour-power exists only as a capacity of the living individual. Its production consequently presupposes his existence. Given the existence of the individual, the production of labour-power consists in his reproduction of himself or his maintenance. For his maintenance he requires a certain quantity of the means of subsistence. Therefore the labour-time necessary for the production of labour-power is the same as that necessary for the production of those means of subsistence; in other words, the value of labour-power is the value of the means of subsistence necessary for the maintenance of its owner. However, labour-power becomes a reality only by being expressed; it is activated only through labour. But in the course of this activity, i.e., labour, a definite quantity of human muscle, nerve, brain, etc. is expended, and these things have to be replaced. Since more is expended, more must be received. If the owner of labour-power works today, tomorrow he must again be able to repeat the same process in the same conditions as regards health and strength. His means of subsistence must therefore be sufficient to maintain him in his normal state as a working individual. His natural needs, such as food, clothing, fuel and housing vary according to the climatic and other physical peculiarities of his country. On the other hand, the number and extent of his so-called necessary requirements, as also the manner in which they are satisfied, are themselves products of history, and depend therefore to a great extent on the level of civilization attained by a country; in particular they depend on the conditions in which, and consequently on the habits and expectations with which, the class of free workers has been formed. In contrast, therefore, with the case of other commodities, the determination of the value of labour-power contains a historical and moral element. Nevertheless, in a given country at a given period, the average amount of the means of subsistence necessary for the worker is a known *datum*." (Karl Marx, *Capital* [New York: Random House, 1977], vol. 1, pp. 274–75.)

To this we can add the observation that the value of women's labor power under capitalism is invariably less than that of men. In the United States this is reflected in the fact that full-time female workers, taken as a whole, receive 59 cents for every dollar earned by full-time male workers. This inequality is part of the "historical and moral element" that Marx refers to in the determination of the value of labor power. It is due to the legacy of women's oppression throughout the history of class society, which is based on women's economic dependence on men. This dependence begins to break down as soon as women begin to be incorporated into the capitalist labor market. But eliminating the historic legacy and creating the social and economic conditions for real equality between men and women can only be accomplished through complete incorporation of women into economic production and the socialization of domestic work. These goals cannot be completely achieved short of the victorious working-class struggle to overturn capitalist property relations on a world scale.

THE STRUGGLE BY WOMEN AGAINST THEIR OPPRESSION AS A SEX IS A FORM OF THE CLASS STRUGGLE

Report adopted by the National Convention of the Socialist Workers Party, August 7, 1979

by Mary-Alice Waters

The draft resolution, "Socialist Revolution and the Struggle for Women's Liberation," submitted by the United Secretariat of the Fourth International for discussion and vote at its 1979 World Congress, is a historic document. As the introduction to the resolution states, "The basic Marxist positions on women's oppression are part of the programmatic foundations of the Fourth International. However, we are discussing and adopting a full resolution on women's liberation for the first time in the international's history. With that in mind, the purpose of the following resolution is to set down our basic analysis of the character of women's oppression, and the place the struggle against that oppression occupies in our perspective for all three sectors of the world revolution. . . ."

The only other time the international Marxist movement has had a similar discussion was in 1921 at the third congress of the Communist International. The "Theses for Propaganda Work Among Women," adopted at that congress, represents the most advanced point reached on this question by the revolutionary workers international prior to today.

As with every resolution, the pioneer "Theses" reflected the historic conditions under which they were drafted. Although they still remained a small minority of the work force, large numbers of women had been drawn into the labor market during the industrial expansion at the end of the nineteenth century, and the beginning of the twentieth. This brought about fundamental changes in the economic and social status of women and led to a series of women's struggles and the "first wave" of feminism.

The Comintern resolution took account of the experiences of its predecessor, the Second International, in building mass women's organizations during the years prior to World War I, its role in the fight for suffrage and other demands, and its attitude toward the various procapitalist women's organizations.

Above all, it drew on the experiences of the Russian revolution and stressed the importance of winning women to the side of the revolution during those first desperate years when, under the leadership of the Bolsheviks, the new workers government in the Soviet Union was fighting for its life.

The Comintern resolution based itself on Marx and Engels's historical materialist analysis of the relationship between women's oppression and class society. It integrated the lessons of the experiences of the workers movement up to that time. And it called on every Communist party, "east and west," to embark on a course of action designed "to awaken the initiative of the woman worker, to eradicate her lack of self-confidence, and in the process of involving her in practical organizational work and struggle, teach her to understand the reality of the fact that every victory of the Communist Party, every action against capitalist exploitation, represents a step forward for women."

A lot has happened since 1921. We had to think through and incorporate the lessons of fifty-eight years of the class struggle in our current draft international resolution on women's liberation.

We have seen not only the results of the victory of the October revolution, with the historic advances it brought for women in such areas as equal rights, child care, abortion, education, and employment, but we have also seen the consolidation of the Stalinist counterrevolution. In the 1930s the Soviet Thermidor drove women back to the status of glorified pack animals. The scientific understanding of women's oppression and the struggle to eradicate it was obliterated, along with the rest of Marxist theory and its revolutionary perspectives.

Stalinism so corrupted Marxism and eclipsed our revolutionary heritage, that in the 1960s, with the new rise of women's struggles and the "second wave" of feminism, even the Fourth International had to begin by reestablishing the materialist foundations that had been laid down by Marx and Engels. We had to catch up to where they had been a hundred years ago, before we could go forward today.

Since 1921, the working class has also gone through the experience of fascism. We have learned the bitter lesson of how this most malignant of all the movements to maintain capitalist rule plays on the fears and insecurities that capitalism generates among women in order to build mass support for reaction.

Since 1921 we have witnessed the upsurge of the colonial revolution, especially sweeping in the post–World War II years, and seen the role of women in the national liberation struggles in countries such as China, Vietnam, Algeria, and Cuba. Most recently we have had the examples of Iran and Nicaragua.

Finally, we have lived through the sweeping economic, social, and cultural changes in the imperialist countries during the Great Depression and in the post–World War II years. We have seen the effects of the incorporation of ever larger numbers of women into the work force as a result of the accelerated expansion of industrial production. These were the changes that gave rise to the massive protests and changes in consciousness accompanying the "second wave" of feminism.

The cadres of the Fourth International today are not only products of, but have also been participants in and leaders of, the past decade of struggles for women's rights. Our experiences and the lessons we have learned went into drafting this document for the World Congress. It is a product of international collaboration at its best. No single section of the Fourth International could have written anything as comprehensive.

To take just one example, the section on "Women's Liberation in the Colonial and Semicolonial World" was drafted primarily by our Iranian and Mexican comrades, who drew on their experiences, contributions of our comrades in India, Puerto Rico, Colombia, and many other countries, as well as the historical lessons of our movement in China.

Moreover, the line of the resolution was put to a demanding test in the events of the Iranian revolution and the role of our comrades in the demonstrations for women's rights that were part of it. They were much better prepared for the struggles that unfolded in Iran this year, better prepared to understand, participate in, and lead them, as a result of the collective international effort that went into drafting this resolution.

No other current in the workers movement or in the feminist movement could have drafted the kind of comprehensive resolution the Fourth International now has before it. And for us it's not simply an intellectual exercise. It is a guide to revolutionary action by the working class and its vanguard, male and female.

It is also the best possible guide for women who may not yet be part of the revolutionary workers movement but are determined to subordinate to nothing the fight for female equality.

A rich discussion

While the draft resolution was adopted unanimously by the United Secretariat of the Fourth International (with one abstention), the discussion in a number of sections indicates there is not unanimity on its general line throughout the international.

Two contributions to the International Internal Discussion Bulletin by comrades of the International Marxist Group, the British section of the Fourth International, point up some of the differences that need to be clarified. "Women's Caucuses Within a Revolutionary Organisation" [IIDB, Vol. XVI, No. 2, May 1979] is a resolution adopted by the last national congress of the IMG. "On the Women's Liberation Resolution," by Harlow [IIDB, Vol. XVI, No. 4, July 1979], "concentrates on reflecting the discussion within the IMG Women's Commission."

I want to take up a number of the points raised in these contributions because they will be helpful in clarifying the line of the document. I hope we can convince the IMG comrades who agree with these contributions to change their minds, because taken as a whole they constitute a different line than that contained in the draft resolution.

There have also been a number of contributions to our preconvention discussion in the SWP, especially on the character of the gay liberation struggle, which relate to the origin and character of women's oppression. I want to discuss some of these contributions as well, because they raise questions that are being discussed throughout the international, and several of them have a line in contradiction to that of the draft resolution.

So this report will concentrate on those points which most need to be clarified in light of the wide-ranging international discussion.

Strategic importance of the struggle for women's liberation

We should begin with the political heart of the document.

The struggle for women's liberation is a form of the class struggle. It occupies a vital place in the strategic line of march of the proletariat toward the establishment of a workers government. For the first time in recorded history, such governments, on a world scale, will place power in the hands of a class that has no material interest in oppressing women. As the structure of society is overhauled from top to bottom, vast revolutionary changes in all social relations will unfold, including the eradication of all aspects of sex inequality that are institutionalized under class domination.

We do not say that the fight for women's liberation is a form of the class struggle only because, or even primarily because the majority of women are today part of the labor market in a few imperialist countries, like the United States. That is something very recent in historical terms. This trend indicates the direction of capitalist economic development. It creates objective conditions more favorable than ever before for the victory of the working class and for women. But the struggle for women's liberation, however episodic and embryonic, was an aspect of the class struggle for millennia prior to the current epoch of capitalism in its death agony.

It is a form of the class struggle because women's oppression itself is a product of class society. It has been an indispensable cornerstone of class society at every stage of its development.

Today, the integration of women into the labor market and, increasingly, into the industrial work force gives the struggle for women's liberation greater strategic importance for the class struggle than ever before. The interrelationship of the struggles of women and those of the organized labor movement is much closer. Understanding that women are both allies of the working class and an increasingly weighty component of the working class is indispensable to mobilizing the allies of the working class; indispensable to unifying the working class and helping to strengthen it politically; indispensable to preparing the working class for the socialist reconstruction of society tomorrow.

Thus, as the resolution explains, labor's strategic line of march must include support for and building of mass women's organizations, fighting for women's demands. This is intertwined with the transformation of the organized labor movement into an instrument of revolutionary struggle and the development of a class-struggle leadership of women and men.

To identify these goals, we must construct a revolutionary party whose proletarian composition includes the necessary component of women and oppressed nationalities.

This same strategic line is reiterated in each of the four documents that are being presented to the 1979 World Congress of the Fourth International by the United Secretariat Majority Caucus. This fact is important because it helps define the character of the turn we are making on a world scale to build proletarian parties whose big majority are industrial workers. It is not a turn away from the allies of labor with the greatest social weight, such as women, but a turn toward the radicalizing young working-class forces that will provide leadership for the struggles of *both* women and the labor movement.

The resolution on "Socialist Revolution and the Struggle for Women's Liberation" is not an optional extra. It is an indivisible part of the Fourth International's line today.

The character of women's oppression

The two most fundamental questions dealt with in the resolution are the origins of women's oppression in the rise of class society with its concomitant family, private property, and state; and the character of this family as an indispensable economic institution of class rule. Those two points are part of the bedrock of Marxism, of a historical-materialist approach to women's oppression—and to all of human history.

If the document failed to deal adequately with the origins of women's oppression and the character of the family system, or if it contained an analysis that was wrong on those two points, the entire political line of the resolution would go wrong. It would open the door to divorcing the struggle for women's liberation from the class struggle.

The origin of women's oppression is not something of interest solely to anthropologists. Nor is it a question that only comrades involved in debates in the women's liberation movement need to be knowledgeable about. Nor is it possible to dismiss it as a historical matter on which we need not take a position. What is at issue involves the most fundamental elements of Marxism, the principles of a materialist conception of history.

The resolution says the following on the origins of women's oppression:

"The oppression of women is not determined by their biology, as many contend. Its origins are economic and social in character. Throughout the evolution of pre-class and class society, women's childbearing function has always been the same. But their social status has not always been that of a degraded domestic servant, subject to man's control and command.

"Before the development of class society, during the historical period that Marxists have traditionally referred to as primitive communism (subsistence societies), social production was organized communally and its product shared equally. There was therefore no exploitation or oppression of one group or sex by another because no material basis for such social relations existed. . . .

"The origin of women's oppression is intertwined with the transition from pre-class to class society. . . . The change in women's status developed along with the growing productivity of human labor . . . and the development of the possibility for some humans to prosper from the exploitation of the labor of others."

To those of us educated in the school of Marx and Engels, that sounds noncontroversial. But there are comrades in the Fourth International who disagree. For example, in the introduction to the contribution by Comrade Harlow, she and Comrade Clynes note that "the debate on the origins of women's oppression is not reflected adequately" in the international resolution.

They are absolutely correct.

In drafting a resolution to guide the work of the Fourth International we did not seek to agnostically "reflect a debate." Our purpose was to take a clear and unequivocal stand on the essential points in dispute.

Some comrades in the international clearly reject the position that is contained in the document on the ground that it merely reaffirms the fundamental foundations elaborated by Marx and Engels more than a hundred years ago. They argue that Marx and Engels's analysis was based on ignorance due to the paucity of anthropological research available to them. These comrades think the Fourth International today will only be discredited by associating itself with Marx and Engels's views.

In reaffirming that the cause of women's oppression is economic and rooted in the development of class society, we are unambiguously rejecting several alternate explanations for the nature of women's oppression.

Four false theories of women's oppression

First, we are rejecting the position that is upheld by radical feminists, like Shulamith Firestone and others, who deny that changes in women's status are determined by women's role in social production. They argue that women have *always* been oppressed because of their biological role in procreation; that women's "oppression goes back beyond recorded history to the animal kingdom itself"; and that the "materialist view of history [is] based on sex itself." [*Dialectic of Sex*, by Shulamith Firestone.]

We reject each thesis of this biological determinism.

Secondly, we are rejecting the position that women's oppression is defined by sex roles or by the psycho-sexual structure of males and females. In the SWP preconvention discussion Comrade Kurt argues that in pre-class society, "members of both sexes were born into roles in much the same way one is born into a social class today." ["In Reply to Cde. Z's Plenum Report on Lesbian/Gay Liberation—Part II," SWP Discussion Bulletin, Vol. 36, No. 22, page 12.]

Membership in a class is not defined by what one does or doesn't do. It is defined by what one owns or doesn't own, by an individual or family's relationship to the means of production. Classes are characterized by institutionalized material inequality, perpetuated from one generation to the next through the family system. That is precisely what did *not* exist during the epoch of primitive communism. The product of all social labor was shared equally. That's why there could be no oppression or exploitation, because no material basis for such social relations existed.

Thirdly, we are rejecting the position that oppression stems from a social division of labor *per se*. Of course, we're in favor of developing the rounded skills and abilities of every individual, of each person learning how to do as many different things as possible. But division of labor *per se* does not give rise to inequality.

If a man knows how to do something that a woman doesn't, does that give him power over her? No. Not unless there is a material advantage, a material inequality, involved, one that is institutionalized and perpetuated through generations by forms of private property. We are not idealists. We do not believe that knowledge equals power equals oppression.

Fourthly, we are rejecting the concept that sex oppression—the oppression of all women as a sex—is equivalent to or even largely defined by *sexual* repression, that is, repression of women's sexuality or of all sexuality. Sexism—that is, all the countless ways in which the economic and social inequality of women in class society is expressed and codified in social mores—is something totally different from what has been called "heterosexism," or judgments about any particular form of sexual activity.

The extreme repression of female sexuality and the related warping and distortion of all sexual relations is a *by-product* of women's *economic* dependence. In other words, sexual repression is a product of class society.

Its original purpose was not, as is often stated, to enable men to ensure the paternity of their offspring. That is an ideological rationalization that came along much later. The function of sexual repression was, and is, to reinforce the social and economic dependence of women on the patriarchal family. On that basis the entire ideological superstructure of the ruling class developed, with the double standard of monogamy for women and almost unrestricted sexual activity for men. Only "thy neighbor's wife"—that is, a married woman of your own ruling class—was not to be "coveted" according to biblical commandment.

Other institutions, such as adultery and prostitution, developed historically as necessary concomitants to the family. All of these grew up on the new economic foundation, institutionalized in the family, where every woman was virtually the private property of a man. That is what the marriage contract was—a property arrangement, a bill of sale. A woman had no rights. She belonged to her father or brother, then to her husband. According to custom, and often sanctioned by law, she could even be murdered by the men of her family for violating their "honor."

Sexual oppression, enforced by such extreme measures, helped keep women in their subordinate place and maintain the stability of the family system. But its efficacy was the *result* of women's economic dependence. Sexual oppression was not the *source* of her degraded status.

While the resolution rejects any biological or nonmaterialist explanation for female inequality and reaffirms the economic origins of women's oppression, it does not ask for a vote on other kinds of historical questions, which remain open to debate and discussion. It simply insists on the fundamental premises of historical materialism.

Class society has not always existed. It had a historical beginning and can be replaced by communism. Likewise women's oppression has not always existed. It had a historical beginning and it too can be replaced by equality of the sexes.

This theoretical foundation underlies our political orientation today and determines our approach to all aspects of the struggle for women's liberation, including our analysis of the character of the women's liberation movement, the program of demands we raise, and why we address them to the ruling class and its agents.

The family system

Closely intertwined with the origins and character of women's oppression is the question of the family. The resolution reaffirms that the family system is an indispensable pillar of class rule. It is the historical mechanism for institutionalizing the social inequality that accompanies the rise of private property and perpetuating class divisions from one generation to the next. The family is first and foremost an *economic* institution that has evolved a great deal as it has adapted to meet the changing needs of ruling classes throughout all stages of class society.

Because the family system is indispensable to the structuring of social inequality, the economic dependence of women and their oppression within the family system is likewise indispensable to class rule. The domestic labor of women in the home provides the least expensive and most ideologically acceptable system of reproducing labor power. It minimizes the proportion of the social surplus consumed in raising each new generation, and maximizes the proportion available for private accumulation. Thus women's oppression is not an inessential or optional feature of class society.

On the question of the family—as with the origin of women's oppression—the resolution firmly rejects a number of false ideas.

Six errors concerning the family

First, we reject the argument that the family system is something that is useful to the ruling class in capitalist society but not necessary. Could capitalism create some other social mechanism to organize the reproduction of labor power and perpetuate class divisions? We say no. It's not possible. Historical materialism precludes that. The family setup, however modified, is indispensable.

Secondly, we reject the idea that there has been any *fundamental* change in the function of the family system under capitalism. Today's urban "nuclear family" may look quite different from the extended farm family of the last century, to say nothing of the family under classical slave society. But the fact that the family is less and less a productive unit does not alter its essential function as the transmission belt for dividing society between those who own the major means of production and those who do not, between the exploiters and the exploited.

Under capitalism the state begins to take over general responsibility for some social tasks previously borne almost exclusively by each individual family—such as education (previously the exclusive privilege of the ruling classes), health care, or social security for the elderly. But such social programs are never designed to *replace* the family. They reinforce it. There is never a doubt that each family bears ultimate responsibility for its own. This becomes most obvious in any period of economic crisis, when cuts in social services brutally shift a growing burden of responsibility back onto the shoulders of each individual family of working people.

Thirdly, the resolution reiterates the discovery made by Marx and Engels more than a century ago that the family is an alien class institution historically imposed on the working class. With the rise of industrial capitalism, as women and children were incorporated into the work force in massive numbers, often working 12- and 14-hour days, the family began disintegrating in the working class. The ruling class consciously intervened to reinforce and strengthen the family in the last quarter of the nineteenth century, because its disintegration was posing a threat to capitalist domination.

The social mechanism for reproducing human beings healthy enough and "socialized" enough to sell their labor power and produce surplus value for a few years was falling apart. For society to take general responsibility for raising and minimally educating children was economically precluded. The costs of such social care could only be taken out of surplus value and thus reduce profits. So the family structure had to be reimposed on the working class.

We reject the position that is advanced by many women in the feminist movement, as well as by some comrades of the Fourth International, that it was male workers who benefited from the introduction of protective legislation that kept women out of many industries in the nineteenth century. Likewise, we reject the argument that male workers have a material stake in the oppression of women in the family and thus benefited from reinforcing the family.

For example, one of the amendments to the international women's liberation resolution proposed by comrades on the Gay Commission of the British International Marxist Group expresses this opinion.

They argue that a sentence should be added

to the resolution stating that efforts to shore up the family in the middle of the last century were "backed up by strong pressures from male workers' organizations. This was based on fear of job competition from women and children; the desire of the male workers for the social benefits of 'family life.'"

This proposed addition is misleading because it implies that in addition to the ruling class the working class as well—or at least male workers—had a historical interest in maintaining the family system.

Fourthly, the resolution makes it clear that the disintegration of the family system is inevitable as capitalism inexorably draws more and more women into the work force. This is evident in the steadily climbing divorce rates in all of the advanced capitalist countries. The family ceases to be a productive unit in the working class, and then begins to disintegrate as every adult member goes out and sells his or her labor power individually on the capitalist labor market. Despite wage differentials and job discrimination, women thereby gain a qualitatively new degree of economic independence. But there is not and there cannot be any alternative to the family system so long as social relations are based on the existence and maintenance of private property.

The disintegration of the family system under capitalism brings great suffering to the masses of working people. In bourgeois society, the contradiction between the romantic mythology surrounding marriage and the reality of personal relations is so acute that—in addition to all the economic hardship that comes with the disintegration of the family—it wreaks emotional and psychological havoc on millions of human beings every year. Many never recover.

We solidarize with those who face such personal misery. But unlike the Stalinists who tell a double lie—about what capitalism has in store for us and about what can be done—we tell the truth. We say there is no way to "save the family." As all institutions of class rule, it will continue to decay and disintegrate because capitalism has outlived its historically progressive role. The relations of production come more and more into conflict with the forces of production.

But until we eradicate the economic system based on private property and eliminate economic compulsion as the bond that corrodes all social relations and prevents them from having a truly human character, the disintegration of the family with all its attendant misery is just one more catastrophe capitalism has in store for us. It is one more reason to fight to get rid of this rotten system. And one more reason to demand a total social security program that covers every aspect of the economic and social needs of working people.

We reject the notion that communes or any other "alternative life-style" offer a *social* alternative under capitalism—even if a few individuals find what they imagine is a tolerable personal solution that way. And insofar as the search for "life-style" alternatives under capitalism becomes a *political* orientation, it is a road *away* from the class struggle and a revolutionary working-class perspective of trying to end the system that is the source of misery for millions.

Fifthly, the resolution stresses the role of the family in molding the character structure, the social and sexual behavior of each new generation. Within the family the attitudes and values that are necessary for survival in class society are inculcated in each individual child—respect for hierarchy and authority, sexual repression, and so forth. This kind of "education" can only be done within the family from the earliest age. There is no economic possibility for it to be accomplished elsewhere under capitalism. In this sense the family plays an indispensable ideological—as well as economic—role. But the "socializing" function is not what fundamentally defines and ultimately shapes the family institution.

Sixthly, we reject the idea that the family is basically a sexual relationship, or that any particular kind of sexual behavior represents a threat to the family system. The disintegration of the family is not the *result* of an evolving "sexual revolution." Changes in sexual mores are the product of greater economic independence of women. It is this growing economic independence that brings about the disintegration of the family and the consequent cultural changes.

The monogamous norm has always been for women only. Only in the last century, with the ideological buttressing of the family institution in order to reimpose it on the working class, has the myth been propagated that most sexual relations take place within the family between husband and wife. Throughout recorded history the opposite has been the case. In the ruling class, sexual relations between husband and wife were for procreation, and most sexual activity, especially for men, was outside of the family.

There is no form of sexual activity—whether it is homosexuality, prostitution, adultery, incest, bestiality, necrophilia, foot fetishism, or anything else—that constitutes or ever constituted a threat to the family institution. That is one of the most commonly held misconceptions in the gay rights movement and sometimes in the women's movement too. It was repeatedly asserted in contributions to the SWP preconvention discussion as though it were an undisputed fact. For example, Comrades Joe and Sandy in their contribution, "In Defense of the Gay Liberation Movement," state: "An end to the oppression of gays and lesbians would weaken the stranglehold of the family on the working class and on women." [SWP DB, Vol. 36, No. 26, p. 40.]

Let's leave aside the implied false premise—that gay and lesbian oppression could be ended under capitalism. The problem with the sentence is that it puts the question on the wrong axis. The primary function of the family is not to control the sexual activity of its members. It is an economic institution. To release its stranglehold you have to alter the property forms encasing the economic foundations on which it rests.

The realization that women's oppression is above all an economic question and that everything else is derivative is the essence of a materialist understanding of that oppression. Without that as your starting point, you will lose your bearings in understanding class society and the class struggle as a whole. Failure to grasp this fact is at the root of the erroneous positions held by many feminists on the question of whose interests are served by women's oppression.

Who benefits from women's oppression?

In his "Reply to Comrade Z . . . Part II," Comrade Kurt argues that Brian Weber's suit against the affirmative-action program at the Kaiser Aluminum plant in Gramercy, Louisiana, may not have been in the interest of the working class as a whole, but it certainly was in Weber's *personal* interest. He thinks Weber has his own material stake in maintaining the oppression of women and Blacks.

Similarly, Comrade Harlow of the IMG argues in her contribution to the International Internal Discussion Bulletin that "male workers especially do have a certain material advantage, for the time being, in discrimination against women." [IIDB Vol. XVI, No. 4, p. 7.]

The paragraph containing that sentence says a number of wrong things. It's worth taking the passage apart sentence by sentence in order to get to the core of the question of who benefits from women's oppression—and what implications the answer to that question has for our perspectives and strategy.

The passage from the contribution by Comrade Harlow says the following:

"The document poses the need for an autonomous organisation of women to fight against the bureaucracy of the workers movement. What is not explained, and is in fact glossed over with statements about the objective interests of the working class being in the fight against women's oppression, is how far the working class as a whole has internalised sexist attitudes towards women. For example on page 9, 3b, the document lists the discrimination that still exists against women in the workforce. It mentions 'sexual aggression of foremen or supervisory personnel.' It does not mention the fact that many male workers not only do not fully support women's struggles but do in fact scab on them. In Britain in 1974 women workers in an engineering factory in Lancashire occupied the factory in the course of a struggle for equal pay. The male workers assisted the management in breaking it although the strike was supported by the union.

"The bureaucracy of the labour movement has no long-term interest in fighting for women's liberation, their interest lies in maintaining capitalism, they will support women's struggles only in so far as it is necessary to retain their position or as it helps them to recruit women to their union. But many rank-and-file members of the working class do not perceive that it is in their interests to fight for women's liberation. Male workers especially do have a certain material advantage, for the time being, in discrimination against women. For example laws which discriminate against women in preventing them from doing night shifts, or working in coal mines, could be supported by male workers, as they were fought for by them, to keep women out of better paid jobs. Many class conscious militants expect their wives to play the traditional role at home, so that they can get on with their trade-union work. Arthur Scargill, one of the best known and most political trade-union leaders in Britain, not only explicitly supports the National Union of Miners paper having a pin-up but his wife is quoted as saying he hardly knows how to make a cup of tea." [IIDB, Vol. XVI, No. 4, pp. 6–7.]

It is correct to say that the bureaucracy of the labor movement has no long-term interest in fighting for women's liberation. But they have no short-term interest, either. Their goal is to maintain the status quo, to accept the divisions and stratifications of the working class fostered by the bosses, and preserve their material privileges by basing themselves on the highest-paid strata of workers. They even weigh organizing more women into the union (with the increased dues income that will bring) against the possible new demands women will make or militancy they might exhibit—that is, a heightened threat to class-collaborationist stability.

Recognizing that the trade-union bureaucracy as a social layer has no interest in—is, in fact, threatened by—the fight for women's liberation, however, doesn't tell you what to do about it. How do we help our fellow workers to see that there is a conflict of interests between them and the bureaucracy which is serving the employers? What is our strategy?

Comrade Harlow argues that the international resolution "poses the need for an autonomous organisation of women to fight against the bureaucracy of the workers movement." That statement, too, is wrong.

Independent women's organizations are needed to mobilize women in struggle against the ruling class, to raise clear and precise demands against the bosses, exposing the class institutions and class interests responsible for maintaining women's oppression. We strive to mobilize the organized labor movement—*including the trade-union bureaucracy*—in support of such demands. In this process we come into conflict with the bureaucracy which acts as the employers' labor-lieutenants. But the union bureaucracy is not a monolithic bloc. It too is stratified. Some layers are closer to the ranks, more susceptible to their pressure. One of the by-products of the struggle for women's demands, if it is correctly oriented and directed against rulers and their agents, will be further openings for the development of a class-struggle leadership, in the unions and in the women's movement. This will be facilitated by a few more divisions within the labor bureaucracy. That is our orientation—not building a women's movement *to fight the bureaucracy.*

Comrade Harlow is correct when she states that "many rank-and-file members of the working class do not perceive that it is in their interests to fight for women's liberation." That holds true for quite a few other areas as well, such as combating racial prejudice, or fighting for a workers government.

But why? What is the cause?

We answer that many workers don't automatically see that women's liberation is in their interests because they are not fully *class* conscious. They're influenced by ruling-class ideology, which inculcates a false consciousness. They think in terms of *I*, not *we*; of me and them, not us.

Comrade Harlow gives a different answer. She says the reason many workers don't see that it is in their class interest to fight for women's liberation is because it is *not* in the immediate interest of all workers. "Male workers especially do have a certain material advantage, for the time being, in discrimination against women." And in the passage already quoted she specifies two areas in which male workers gain special privileges from discrimination against women.

First they are able to keep women out of better paying jobs.

Second, male workers gain a material advantage from the fact that women do the housework.

What is fundamentally wrong with this argument that male workers have a material stake in women's oppression?

Any individual male worker may have a better chance of getting a particular job if women are excluded from competition, or may have a few hours of leisure for himself some evening if his wife feeds the kids and puts them to bed. As long as he thinks in individual terms, as long as he thinks in terms of *me,* and as long as he thinks "the time being" is permanent (and thus capitalism is permanent), he can falsely conclude that he is better off because women are oppressed. But is this objectively true?

We say no. That individual male belongs to a class whose interests, both short-term and long-term, are diametrically opposed to the oppression of women, because women's oppression divides the working class and shifts the relationship of class forces to the advantage of the bosses. This has negative consequences on the wages, working conditions, etc., of all workers—that is, on their immediate interests as well as their long-term ones.

If what one sometimes falsely believes to be in one's immediate personal interests were in the long run more compelling than the historic interests of classes, then Marxism would have no validity whatsoever. If that were true we should have closed up shop a long time ago. What basis would there ever be for united action by the working class? Why should there be industrial rather than craft unions? Why shouldn't everyone try to make foreman? Why should workers of the world unite?

We are the first to recognize that every worker does not correctly identify his or her class interest on every question every day. The contradiction between the objective needs and the subjective understanding of the class and its components is acute. But it can be overcome, especially in periods of sharpening class conflict. Then the overwhelming majority of workers will begin to see where their real interests lie, not primarily because we tell them, but through their own experiences. In the heat of the class struggle they can rapidly become convinced that their personal interests and class interests coincide. It can be pointed out: Aren't you better off if both husband and wife can get jobs as auto workers, steelworkers, or miners? If you both join with other workers to use your organized power to fight for adequate child care and other social services? Isn't that in your immediate personal interests?

This is crucially important. It underlies our proletarian strategy for women's liberation. Our enemy is not male workers—although individuals can wander into the enemy camp ideologically (and in personal practice) for a shorter or longer period of time, and they have to be dealt with accordingly. But it is the boss class and its agents who consciously strive to deepen the antagonisms between male and female workers, between male workers and their wives, because that weakens the solidarity and unity of the class.

Not only is it the bosses who *benefit* from discrimination against, and harassment of, women on the job; it is also the bosses and foremen who hold the real *power* over women, not male workers. For example, sexual harassment of a woman worker by a foreman is backed up by his control over whether she keeps her job.

That is why our fire is aimed at the foreman and the supervisors. That is how we pressure and divide the trade-union officials and win over fellow workers.

We know that many male workers (and female workers too) have deep sexist prejudices, and often express them in words and deeds. Our attitude is not to let such actions pass without challenge, but we try to counter them in such a way that we educate fellow workers to understand that they are simply doing the boss's job for him if they give women a hard time and do not treat them as equals.

Women will learn from their own experiences how to deal with these problems in the framework of the correct proletarian strategy, tactically applied in light of the real relationship of forces on the job and the needs of the class struggle as a whole.

Comrade Harlow objects to the sentences in the international resolution that mention the problems women often face on the job from sexual harassment by foremen or supervisory personnel. She says: "What is not explained, and is in fact glossed over with many statements about the objective interests of the working class being in the fight against women's oppression, is how far the working class as a whole has internalised sexist attitudes towards women." The document "mentions 'sexual aggression of foremen or supervisory personnel.' It does not mention the fact that many male workers not only do not support women's struggles, but do in fact scab on them."

The resolution rejects that kind of "balanced" approach. It is wrong, because it fails to distinguish who gains from the harassment of women on the job, whose interests are served. It doesn't take as its starting point the fact that women's oppression is a form of class oppression and a condition for exploitation. Thus it does not orient us towards a correct strategy for winning women's liberation. We don't have a dual axis for our demands or our struggle. We don't have one set of demands against the bosses and the ruling class, and another which is directed against men or male workers. That would be suicidal.

Relations between men and women in class society are always unequal. That's simply a fact of life. But we don't propose to equalize them by forcing men today to "give up" their "privileges." Our objective is not to shift the *social* burdens women bear from individual women to individual men. We want *society* to shoulder the responsibilities thrust on each individual family, and above all on women within it.

Any other approach amounts to *substituting* the search for better personal relations today for charting a political course for our class.

On a personal level, we are all for men sharing the burdens of household drudgery. That's what we do in our own lives. We exert great social pressure on male comrades to conduct themselves in accord with our political program and support for women's liberation.

But that cannot be a substitute for a political strategy to change society, to advance the class struggle, to raise the class consciousness of millions.

Moreover, as proletarian revolutionists, we do not base our political judgment of people on their personal relations or sexual habits. We don't care whether Arthur Scargill can make a cup of tea or not. Maybe Lenin didn't know how to cook either. And what about Marx? How many times have we heard even "socialist-feminists" tell us that Marxism is an insufficient theoretical framework for understanding women's oppression—and argue that Marx's personal relations with women and his own family prove that his analysis must have been politically wrong?

Affirmative action

What is our political strategy for raising the class consciousness of male and female workers? In addition to the demands we advance for basic democratic rights such as legal equality, abortion, and others, we put forward basically two axes of struggle.

1. We concretize our demands for socializing the domestic labor of women—such as child care.
2. We demand preferential action programs for women in education, employment, job training, in order to break down the barriers that have kept women out of sectors of the economy traditionally restricted to males.

The fight for preferential programs, for affirmative action, plays a decisive role in effecting changes in consciousness on a mass scale. It undercuts the divisions and stratifications that are used to hold down the wages and working conditions of all workers. Male and female workers can be convinced that it *is* in their class interest to fight for such demands.

Secondly, the fight for affirmative action makes both men and women more conscious of all the ways in which discrimination against women is built into this society. Oppression is not an idea or a state of mind, it is a social relation. It has material consequences in unequal conditions of life and labor, and deliberate measures are needed in all areas to overcome the results of centuries of oppression of women.

Thirdly, affirmative-action victories begin in the most fundamental way to undercut sexist attitudes toward women. As women break down the social barriers of their second-class status, they gain self-confidence. Men begin to see their women co-workers as equal human beings. They learn to respect and judge women more as people and less as female sex-objects. That has a powerful impact on the attitudes and conduct of millions of men and women in their personal lives. Men *do* start sharing the housework.

It is by charting this kind of *political* course of broad mass struggle for affirmative action and other demands that we seek to break through the false consciousness that's engendered by the ruling class. It is along this path that we help the working class to think socially and act politically, and thereby become more *class* conscious.

Mass independent women's organizations have a vital role to play in helping to advance in this direction. Their actions can converge with progress by vanguard workers in transforming the labor movement and forging the kind of working-class leadership that is necessary for women's struggles.

This brings us to the next point we need to take up—the nature of the women's movement today.

The character of the women's liberation movement

What does the document say about the character of the women's liberation movement? Its main points are the following:

1. "The oppression of women as a sex constitutes the objective basis for the mobilization of women in struggle through their own organizations."

2. "By the women's movement we mean all the women who organize themselves at one level or another to struggle against the oppression imposed on them by this society." At any one time this takes many and diverse organizational forms—consciousness-raising groups, neighborhood groups, student groups, trade-union committees, action coalitions—whatever. ". . . all these are facets of the turbulent and still largely unstructured reality called the independent or autonomous women's movement."

3. "By independent or autonomous we do not mean independent of the needs of the working class. We mean that the movement is organized and led by women; that it takes the fight for women's rights and needs as its first priority, refusing to subordinate that fight to any other interests; that it is not subordinate to the decisions or policy needs of any political tendency or any other social group; that it is willing to carry through the fight by whatever means and together with whatever forces prove necessary."

4. "The dominant organizational form of the women's liberation movement has been all-female groups. . . . This expresses the determination of women to take the leadership of their own organizations in which they can learn and develop and lead. . . ."

5. "The mass women's liberation movement we strive to build must be basically working-class in composition and leadership." This is not for some abstract moral reason but because of the nature of the class struggle. "Only such a movement will be able to carry the struggle for women's liberation through to the end in an uncompromising way, allying itself with the social forces whose interests parallel and intersect those of women. Only such a movement will be able to play a progressive role under conditions of sharpening class polarization."

6. "In this long-term perspective, struggles by women in the unions and on the job have a special importance, reflecting the interrelationship of the women's movement and the workers movement and their impact on each other."

Here, too, Comrade Harlow and others of the IMG Women's Commission raise some important issues that help clarify the line of the resolution.

They object that the document does not adequately spell out the relationship of the women's liberation movement to the class struggle in the one particular paragraph that defines the political character of the women's movement (point 3 above).

That criticism sounds a hollow chord since the resolution does nothing *but* spell out the interrelationship of the struggle for women's liberation and the class struggle for almost thirty pages.

Comrade Harlow's second objection is to the sentence saying that the women's liberation movement we seek to build must be increasingly working-class in composition and leadership. She says that is a sociological definition of the movement which could imply that we do not support the women's liberation movement *unless* it is working-class in composition and leadership.

This objection, too, can be easily disposed of. Nowhere does the resolution imply such an attitude. Moreover, as far as the SWP is concerned, our record in the women's liberation movement should certainly eliminate any lurking doubts in this regard.

But there is more to the matter. We insist on the *class* composition of the women's movement that we strive to build, that *must* be built. It is not a question of individuals. We are not saying that only working-class women can be leaders or that we don't want women of petty-bourgeois or bourgeois origins in the movement. They, too, are oppressed as women and we strive to win them to support and fight uncompromisingly for demands that are in the interests of women's liberation.

But, as the resolution states, only a movement that is basically working-class in composition and leadership will be able to take correct stands under the pressures of deepening class conflict and chart a political course to carry the struggle for women's liberation through to the end as part of the forces fighting for a workers government. This guideline can hardly be contested by Marxists.

The third point that Comrade Harlow thinks is unclear is the nature of the *autonomous* or *independent* women's movement. What is the feminist movement, she asks?

The word "independent" can be confusing. It can mean different things to different people. That's why the resolution defines it precisely and clearly as a political concept. Independent does not mean independent of the class struggle or the interests of the working class. Nor does it mean that some particular organizational form is decisive. What defines the independent women's movement is its political goal. It puts forward the fight for women's needs as its specific aim which it subordinates to no other; it is consistent and uncompromising in its struggle; it aims to be a mass movement collaborating with allies who prove themselves worthy.

Comrade Harlow defines "autonomous" differently. She says that the women's movement is "autonomous from men and from political organisations." The international resolution, on the other hand, insists that the independent women's liberation movement is defined not by the gender of its participants but by its political function.

It is important to sort out several different things.

As the resolution says, we support and help build all-female women's liberation groups. We think that women have the right to use the form of women-only organization to advance their struggle. These groups can play an important role in developing women's self-confidence and mobilizing women in struggle. But such organizations are not synonymous with the women's liberation movement.

That movement is much broader. It's not only women in all-female organizations. It does not exclude men who support our demands, build actions, participate in coalitions. For example, should we conclude that the National Organization for Women in the United States is not part of the independent women's movement just because membership in NOW is also open to men?

The real issue is posed clearly in another way. Comrade Harlow seems to imply that trade-union committees on women's rights which, she points out, are often set up by the bureaucracy to "head off" activity by women, are not legitimately part of the autonomous women's movement because they "do not reflect any understanding for the need of the self organisation of women."

She seems dubious about the resolution's assertion that women's rights committees in the unions stand at the intersection of the women's liberation movement and the labor movement, and if properly led can show the way forward for both.

Other comrades in the Fourth International argue explicitly that while we are not opposed to official women's committees in the unions, they are not part of the women's liberation movement, because they are not independent of male-dominated organizations—the unions! There are often clauses in union statutes which say that all union committees must be open to participation by all members—meaning union brothers could participate in women's rights committees. Thus, these groups are not autonomous from men. Therefore, they are not part of the women's liberation movement.

Such a definition of the women's liberation movement is explicitly rejected in the international resolution.

This helps to clarify one of the questions that has come up in the SWP preconvention discussion. A number of comrades objected to the assertion, made in the April 1979 National Committee plenum report on the gay liberation struggle, that the gay rights movement cannot be defined on the basis of sexuality; it is not composed, we say, only of individuals who sleep with others of the same sex. Some comrades thought we were using a new criterion for the gay liberation movement, different from the way we defined the women's liberation movement or the Black liberation movement.

That is false. We have always defined what the women's liberation movement is by political criteria, not by sex. That does not negate our support for the right of gays, or women, or oppressed nationalities to get together in their own organizations to fight their common oppression. But the totality of such organizations is not synonymous with the gay rights movement, the Black liberation movement, or the women's liberation movement. To adopt any other stance would be hopelessly apolitical and sectarian.

Gender or nationality or religion or sexual orientation are the basis on which individuals are identified as part of social groups that are oppressed in capitalist society. But that tells you nothing about *why* they are oppressed or the character of the struggle that must be waged to end that oppression.

For example, Blacks are not oppressed *because of* the color of their skin, or any other biological characteristic. That is simply how they are identified as a distinct group of human beings. But the *reason* they are oppressed has nothing to do with skin color. Blacks are discriminated against because national oppression plays a crucial economic role under capitalism, dividing the working class and creating a pariah labor pool. You have to understand the origin and character of national oppression if you're going to chart a course of struggle to uproot that oppression.

Likewise, it tells you very little to say that women are oppressed because they are women. The only thing that defines women as distinct from men is a genetic structure which results in a biological role in procreation different from men's. But that is not *why* women are oppressed. Women are discriminated against because their oppression as a sex plays an indispensable economic role in class society.

In the same way, it's false to say, as some comrades have, that gays are oppressed because of their "sexuality" or sexual orientation. That is what defines gays or lesbians as a distinct group, it is not *why* they are oppressed.

Gays are oppressed because the maintenance of *women's* oppression demands the repression of all public sexual behavior (and all private sexual behavior that may become public knowledge) not in conformity with the patriarchal monogamous family system. But, as we saw before, sexual oppression is a subsidiary aspect of women's oppression.

Thus, it would be false to conclude that, since gays are oppressed because of their sexual orientation, therefore to end their oppression they must organize a movement for sexual freedom. That would entail a total misunderstanding of the interrelationship of gay oppression, women's oppression, and class society.

We say the struggle against gay oppression must be a political struggle, directed against the institutionalized ways in which that oppression is effected, the material sanctions used by state authorities to keep gays in their closets—such as discrimination in housing, employment, child custody, tolerance of police brutality, etc.

'Sexual freedom' and class struggle

A counterorientation—denying that the axis of the gay liberation struggle is a political movement for democratic rights—was clearly outlined in a recent article by David Thorstad, a leader of the North American Man-Boy Love Association, in the newspaper the *Guardian*. In it he argues that "the struggle for sexual freedom is an integral part of the overall struggle to overthrow capitalism." Elsewhere he talks about "capitalism and its heterosexist dictatorship." He seems to think the two categories are of equal nature and importance.

In a like vein Comrades F and H argue in the SWP preconvention discussion bulletin that the goal of the gay liberation movement is sexual liberation, that its purpose "is to allow all human sexual potential to be released in people."

This is not a new idea, either. Some pre-Marxian Utopian socialists brought forward similar ideas. The anarchist movement at the turn of the century championed free love as an important aspect of the class struggle. The sex-pol movement led by Wilhelm Reich and others in Germany and Austria in the 1930s developed the idea that capitalism could not long survive if the authoritarian character structure of individuals was eroded through modifications in their sexual lives.

The Stalinists assailed Reich as well as Freud for their pioneering contributions to scientific research on sexual repression and human psychology. Reich was expelled from the German Communist Party in 1933. The Trotskyist movement, on the other hand, considered the work of Freud, Reich, and others in the psychoanalytic movement important contributions to science and materialism. But we always rejected the idea that the struggle for sexual freedom is or can ever be an axis of political struggle against capitalism.

It is true that sexual repression is indispensable to class society. But it does not follow that you can undermine capitalism by convincing people to stop repressing their sexual drives or demanding the "right" to freer sexuality.

The liberation of human sexuality from the distortions produced by class society will only come about through the deepest fundamental economic and social changes opened up as a result of the socialist revolution. Along the way, there are certain *political* struggles—such as the right of women and youth to sex education; contraception and abortion; decent, low-cost housing that can offer privacy and a room of one's own; an end to discriminatory laws; affirmative action. The by-product of victorious struggles around such issues can be the elimination of elements of sexual repression and distortion. But a struggle for "sexual freedom" in the abstract will never affect the economic power and institutions of the capitalist class.

As Trotsky points out in *Problems of Everyday Life*, there's tremendous interest in the working class in questions of sex and family relations. When party propagandists organized meetings in the working-class districts of major cities after the October revolution to discuss questions of sex and family life, thousands of people flocked to them.

Of course. Why would one expect anything else? Given the degree to which every individual suffers from the warping and distortion of all sexual relations in class society, everyone is interested in sex. It's safe to say that there's not a single individual who isn't in favor of a more satisfying sex life.

If the All-African People's Revolutionary Party could get 4,000 people to march through the streets of Washington last year demanding "Scientific Socialism," think about what could be done with the demand, "We Want Better Sex!"

The problem is, to whom do you address that demand?

I don't think Congress can help us much. And the good Baptist in the White House who admits to the lust in his heart won't be able to do any better.

More radical critiques of sexual repression are not necessarily synonymous with a deeper political understanding of how to eradicate the economic and social conditions that give rise to sexual repression. If there are fewer restrictions in sexual activity today than ten years ago, or fifty years ago, it is not because people demanded better sex, but because of the qualitative changes in the economic independence of women. Because women are increasingly able to walk away from family relations that are personally intolerable and survive, there are fewer sexual taboos for men and women.

Overriding concern for "sexual freedom" takes those preoccupied with it away from politics, away from the class struggle. And it opens the door to reactionary ideas as well.

Sexual repression is not a mere internal suppression of a biological urge. It results in deep distortions of that urge in ways that flow from the structure and functioning of the family. These distortions of sexuality exist in all of us in one form and to one degree or another. Usually the most destructive compulsions are kept in check through repression.

We can confidently expect that a socialist society, through the socialization of the functions now performed by the family, will eventually produce new men and women free of such distortions. But to demand total freedom of expression for all human sexual potential today means freedom to express all the present distortions of sexuality, many of which are violent and destructive to other individuals. Society must attempt to control them until they "wither away" among the future generations living in a classless society. Rape, child abuse, and extreme forms of sadistic-masochistic compulsion are obvious examples.

This is also relevant to the current debate about "age of consent laws." The issue involved is not the right of teenagers to engage in sexual activity, but the demand by adults who are afflicted with a compulsion to have sex with children to have the right to do so. This is antisocial because it harms children. It is reactionary because it attempts to inflict upon future generations the sicknesses of the present. It is a "sexual potential" which society—capitalist or socialist—must block until such distortions are a thing of humanity's past.

The various ideas about fighting to release all human sexual potential that are prevalent in the gay rights movement (and to a lesser degree in the women's movement) are closely related to counterculturalist currents and proponents of liberation-through-life-style. They are the opposite of our orientation, which approaches the solution to these problems as political issues in the class struggle.

As the international resolution explains:

"We are concerned with all aspects of women's oppression. However, as a political party based on a program that represents the historic interests of the working class and all the oppressed, our prime task is to help direct the women's liberation movement toward political action that can effectively lead to the eradication of private property in which that oppression is rooted. Around every facet of women's oppression we strive to develop demands and actions that challenge the social and economic policies of the bourgeoisie and point toward the solutions that would be possible were it not for the fact that all social policies are decided on the basis of maximizing private profits."

The revolutionary proletarian party we must build

The final question we need to clarify is the character of the revolutionary workers party, including the role of women within the party and the development of women leaders. In the SWP we have given a lot of thought to this question. It has been discussed extensively at National Committee plenums and conventions of the party. The same issue has been raised in virtually every section and sympathizing organization of the Fourth International.

We all recognize that building revolutionary proletarian parties with a sizable cadre of women and with a significant component of women in the central leadership is not a moral question. It is a matter of practical revolutionary politics. Given the accelerating changes in the economic and social role of women, their increasing integration in the work force, if we fail to build workers parties of that kind, we will not be adequately equipped to lead the proletarian forces who will make the socialist revolution in our countries.

The fact that women are drawn into both the labor market and industry in growing numbers also creates the objective conditions that enhance our ability to forge the kinds of parties we need. But the process is not automatic. We are challenged to overcome within our own ranks the divisions and stratifications that exist in the working class; to weld the most conscious elements of our class into an experienced cadre whose confidence in each other is based on proven commitment to our program and loyalty to the party based on that program; to forge that cadre, in the heat of the class struggle, into a homogeneous, tested, self-confident leadership.

That is our task. But helping women comrades to overcome the special obstacles they face poses additional challenges for us. They must be consciously met by the party. We must lead on this question as on others.

This is the context in which the question of organizing women's caucuses had come up in a number of sections of the Fourth International.

Such caucuses are internal meetings of women comrades from which all male comrades are excluded. They are always motivated on the premise that women comrades need to get together to discuss the special problems that women in the party face.

Women's liberation work fractions are a totally different kind of formation. Fractions are set up for a political purpose—to build the party through our intervention in the women's liberation movement, the trade unions, action coalitions, etc.

They move outward into arenas of activity. Women's caucuses, on the other hand, are always directed inward—to discuss what some exclusive subgroup of comrades think is wrong with the party.

Within the Socialist Workers Party the question of women's caucuses has not been a big issue. We discussed and settled that problem at the very beginning of our participation in the women's liberation movement. At that time, a number of comrades suggested that we should organize consciousness-raising discussion groups among women in the party. We clarified why such formations are detrimental—why they create greater obstacles rather than aid in building the party.

Nonetheless, a number of comrades in the SWP have asked if women's caucuses might not be beneficial in some sections of the Fourth International where the kinds of norms and traditions we have in the SWP don't exist.

The international women's liberation resolution says no, unequivocally. Closed internal caucuses based on something other than political criteria are in contradiction with the very character of a Leninist organization, a revolutionary proletarian party. They run counter to our democratic norms. They undermine our centralism in action. And over time, they inevitably begin to affect our program and orientation.

A proposed amendment to the international resolution which would have changed the section rejecting caucuses and taken a positive attitude toward them instead was defeated by a substantial majority of the United Secretariat.

What exactly does the resolution say on this question?

First, the document points out that many of our sections were slow to respond in a revolutionary way to the rise of the women's liberation movement. This failure to understand the revolutionary potential of the women's liberation movement, the incomprehension and insensitivity to obstacles that women comrades face, and the sexist attitudes that lay behind many of these political errors by the leadership produced great frustration and anger among many women comrades. This gave rise to demands by women that they should have the right to caucus by themselves. In other words, the leadership, including the international leadership, failed to politically lead the women's liberation work and that's where we assign responsibility for the errors that were made.

Secondly, the resolution explains why we often support women's caucuses in other organizations in the workers movement, like reformist parties in which we may be doing fraction work or sometimes in trade unions. Yet we are against such caucuses within the revolutionary workers party. The resolution explains why this difference is drawn, why it is not a contradiction.

The reason is very straightforward. Only a Leninist party is based on a program that represents the interests of the working class—that is the political basis of its revolutionary centralism—and functions according to the norms of internal democracy. That makes us qualitatively different from every other formation within the workers movement.

Within the sections and sympathizing organizations of the Fourth International, whatever our weaknesses, errors, and problems may be, we're not confronted with a materially privileged bureaucracy, defending a program that represents the interests of a class other than the working class. There may be conflicts, tensions, and political mistakes, but there's no inherent contradiction between the program of the Fourth International, democratically-elected and controlled leadership bodies, the ranks of our parties, and the needs of the entire working class.

We all stand on the Marxist program, which expresses the generalized interests of the working class. It expresses our common historic class need to overcome the deep cleavages fostered by the rulers to divide our class.

On the basis of that single common program, we have one class of membership: those who agree with that program, loyally build the party, and collaborate with others in a disciplined way to achieve the program. Every single member has an equal right and an equal responsibility to participate in a democratic way to discuss, decide upon, and implement that program. Concretely, this means that every single internal meeting must be organized democratically. Every internal meeting must be organized according to political criteria—fractions according to political work, tendencies or factions according to political agreement. Every member thus qualified must have the possibility to participate, to make her or his opinions known, and to have equal opportunity to influence decisions. There can be no nonpolitical barriers to equal participation—such as exclusion of some comrades on the basis of race, sex, age, educational level, language, class origin, or whatever. That would stand in contradiction to our program and the organizational norms that flow from our program. It would cut across our ability to accomplish our most basic task, the forging of a politically homogenous combat party of workers, not a federation of caucuses, each with its own nuance of programmatic differences and conflicting campaign priorities.

Any decision reached under pressure from groupings not constituted on such a democratic basis will not be able to command disciplined implementation either. Only on the basis of democratic functioning can decisions carry authority.

For these reasons the international women's liberation resolution states that the organization of inner-party caucuses—Black caucuses, women's caucuses, Chicano, gay, lesbian, or short people caucuses—never advance the construction of a Leninist party.

This assessment has also been borne out in practice in those sections of the Fourth International that have gone through the experience of women's caucuses in recent years. Far from helping to correct the political errors or develop the women comrades as self-confident political leaders, the caucuses have had the opposite effect. They deepened the feelings of isolation, conflict, the helplessness. It could not be otherwise because by the very nature of the caucuses they were divorced from the only real context in which progress could be made—organizing the right kind of political work to educate and build the party through women's liberation work in the mass movement.

Thus the caucuses unfortunately deepened the miseducation of comrades, reinforced political errors, fostered cliquism, rationalized gossip, promoted adaptation to the petty-bourgeois feminist milieu in which we were functioning, and accelerated the loss of literally hundreds of women comrades. In light of these experiences a number of sections have reconsidered their previous positions and are now in agreement with the line of the international resolution.

The International Marxist Group is one of the sections which still thinks women's caucuses are correct and serve a useful function. The resolution adopted by the IMG national conference a year ago codifies the right of women to caucus on every single level of the organization, from the political committee to the branches and fractions. This resolution submitted to the international discussion bulletin states, *"The struggle against sexism within our own ranks is the counterpart of the struggle against sexism in the working class."* It projects the need *"to develop the struggle against sexism within the IMG."* [IIDB, Vol. XVI, No. 2, pp. 5–6. Emphasis in original.]

I think those statements express the heart of the error. They assume a fundamental conflict of interest between male and female comrades. If that were true, it would be impossible ever to arrive at a common program for women's liberation and for the working class as a whole. Each sector of the oppressed and exploited would have to wage a fight against the others while at the same time conducting its own separate fight against the ruling class. There would be no need for a revolutionary proletarian party—and also not much objective possibility for victory over the ruling class.

But even if you thought the conflict between men and women in the party could be modified by educating *men,* the "struggle against sexism" would still have to take a *political* form—not an organizational one (caucuses) or a personal one (accusations of sexist behavior that are not taken through normal disciplinary channels). Politically, we would still have to determine what the organization should be doing differently to advance the fight for women's liberation. What political errors are we making because of sexist attitudes?

This will stand out more clearly in the light of an analogy. Sexism is not the only alien class pressure that comes down on a revolutionary party. We're surrounded by all kinds of bourgeois pressures and petty-bourgeois concepts that constitute as deadly a peril to the party as sexism. But how do we deal with petty-bourgeois pressures? Do we organize a proletarian caucus composed of all comrades working in industry, or of all comrades of working-class origins, to "develop the struggle against petty-bourgeois pressures in the organization"?

If there really is a problem of this kind, it shows up in the *program,* in our political *program,* in our political orientation, in what we are doing as an organization. Then we organize politically—in a tendency or a faction, if necessary, to correct the concrete political errors. Any other approach destroys the very foundation of a Leninist organization.

The international resolution recognizes that the problems which have given rise to demands for women's caucuses are real. Antiwoman prejudices in this society are very deep. Economic changes are bringing about alterations, but attitudes in our parties will not be decades ahead of general social conditions, customs, and habits. The course we chart to resolve the internal problems of building proletarian revolutionary parties is a political course. Not a personal or sexual battle between men and women.

We can begin this task of setting the entire international on the correct political course with the resolution on women's liberation that we are discussing, adopting, and implementing.

We send our cadres into the women's liberation movement and integrate the fight for women's needs and demands into all aspects of our work—in the trade unions, in the Black movement, wherever we are. We organize fractions of the party to carry out this work, which is led by the elected political leadership.

We systematically educate our entire membership to understand women's oppression and be knowledgeable about the history of the struggle against it.

We take conscious leadership measures to encourage women and help them overcome the additional obstacles they face.

And, most importantly, we are consciously proletarianizing our parties, getting our members including our women comrades, into industry, which will heighten the self-confidence of our own ranks.

All these questions are being debated throughout the Fourth International in preparation for the 1979 World Congress. One thing we can be sure of is that through this discussion the entire international Trotskyist movement will emerge stronger and more capable of meeting the challenges we face. The fact that we are discussing and adopting such a resolution in a source of revolutionary optimism for us.

The new rise of the women's movement on a world scale has already meant a qualitative strengthening of the revolutionary potential of the working class. It has reinforced the cadres of the Marxist movement. For our class, for women, for the Fourth International, the prospects are much greater today because of this development.

The goal of our struggle is to build a combat party capable of leading the workers to expropriate the bourgeoisie and put an end to a social system that's based on inequality, oppression, and exploitation. That will open the door to move toward freeing all human relations from the shackles of economic compulsion and to create a world in which each human being can develop her or his full creative capacities for the good of all.

The rise of the women's liberation movement brings that day closer.

SUMMARY

One central thing we are trying to accomplish in the current discussion is to place our understanding of the oppression of women as a sex, and the interrelated but quite distinct question of sexual repression, on a firm materialist foundation. We have to understand where these problems come from and what their interrelationship is before we can chart a political course of struggle to change them.

Proceeding from materialist foundations, we will be properly equipped to appreciate all the complexities of women's oppression.

For example, on the question of the family and sexual repression, we emphasize the fact that women's oppression is *economic*, that the family is an *economic* institution of class rule. We state this insistently, precisely because there's so much confusion on this score, and so many feminists and others think that other factors are primary. But once we get ourselves clear, we'll have little trouble in appreciating the value of contributions made by others who are trying to understand the various aspects of bourgeois ideology which reinforce women's oppression. We can then place all the sexual and psychological aspects of oppression in proper perspective.

A materialist understanding of sexuality and sexual repression has, of course, its own importance. For example, I think many of the writings by Wilhelm Reich when he was a Marxist are valuable. His works such as *The Mass Psychology of Fascism* and *The Imposition of Sexual Morality* are serious materialist attempts to deal with significant questions. But if you substitute psychology for political economy as a guide, then you go off base. You'll never be able to chart a class-struggle course toward the establishment of a workers government.

The fact that bourgeois ideology and sex mores have less of a hold on the working class today is extremely important. One comrade made the point in the discussion that gay-baiting and lesbian-baiting are simply not so effective a means of inciting antagonism and division within the working class as before. These changes in consciousness, which are partly due to the role of the gay liberation movement, strengthen the working class. This is significant.

But when it comes down to thinking out a proletarian political strategy, we start from the understanding that ideological shifts on a mass scale *follow* from profound economic and social changes, not vice versa. You can't change the world unless you understand why the world is the way it is.

I want to return to the discussion we've been having on the question of counterculturalism and life-stylism.

The counter political resolution, submitted by the six comrades in Miami, Florida, argues that we should have a positive attitude toward the growth of counterculturalism and life-stylism because it is a sign of deepening radicalization and rejection of bourgeois values.

That is politically wrong.

Such social and cultural phenomena are sometimes signs of a deepening radicalization. We agree. They are also sometimes signs of a downturn in the class struggle, a growing demoralization and loss of perspective.

In neither case do we have *a priori* a positive attitude toward them politically.

Simply rejecting the existing social values and norms doesn't necessarily put you on a revolutionary, class-struggle course. Some who get caught up in counterculturalism and alternative life-styles are taking a first step toward revolutionary politics. But many more are at best on a road out of politics, and at worst moving toward a totally reactionary, anti-working-class orientation. That is why we consider counterculturalism and life-stylism a deadly enemy politically. Only those who can be broken from it will ever be won to a proletarian, Leninist strategy of party building.

On the question of women's caucuses, I'm glad that the comrade spoke and explained the thinking of some of the IMG comrades. The points she made about the general atmosphere and attitudes that exist internally in many sections of the Fourth International are valid. They *are* an obstacle to the political development of women—and every other comrade, I might add.

But women's caucuses still do not provide the solution. Instead of charting a political course of party-building action, intervention in the mass movement, winning comrades to that political perspective, and educating everyone through their own experiences in the process—the women's caucuses tend to turn comrades in on themselves. They foster a relationship of conflict and antagonism—women against the party—rather than a feeling of responsibility for leading the party. They increase cliquism.

They tend to make the women comrades feel ghettoized within the party. We all understand how deep these problems are, but if we're talking primarily to ourselves we will not be able to lead the party forward.

If our approach inside the party begins from *us* and *them*, rather than from *we*, working together to solve the problems that exist, that only deepens the frustrations of the women comrades and their feelings of hopelessness. That is why caucuses don't help to keep women comrades in the party but, as we have seen, accelerate a trajectory away from the party.

A number of comrades made good contributions on the experiences of women in industry. We are learning a great deal as we turn our entire membership toward the political openings in the industrial working class, and begin to mobilize powerful new forces in the fight for women's needs. As Comrade Allio noted, we will want to take a new look at the international resolution when we do the final editing after the world congress. In light of our experiences in industry internationally, we can be more concrete about some points which were abstractions for us when the resolution was drafted a year and a half ago.

Let me comment on two questions.

First, we don't minimize the degree of sexism or prevalence of sexist attitudes among our male fellow workers. Comrades have to deal with this every day on the job. We don't just let such things pass. But we respond in ways that will advance the social and political—the *class*—consciousness of our co-workers. We chart a political course aimed at demonstrating to others that it is the bosses and the ruling class who instigate and benefit from sexist harassment of women workers. Rather than making the union or its leadership the *target* of attacks, we fight to enlist the union and its leadership in the fight to defend women's rights. It is along these lines that we will have the greatest impact in helping to advance labor's consciousness and developing a new proletarian leadership that will fight for women's rights as well as other things.

Second, our turn to industry dovetails with what we are trying to accomplish through the international women's liberation resolution and report—that is, to solidify our understanding of the material roots of women's oppression and deepen our grasp of historical materialism in general. If the heart of Marxism is essentially the generalized interests of the working class, then we are in a better position to understand it, to absorb it, and make its ideas more vivid and relevant as we become a more proletarian party. That process was clearly reflected in the discussions today.

SOCIALIST REVOLUTION AND THE STRUGGLE FOR WOMEN'S LIBERATION
Resolution adopted by the National Convention of the Socialist Workers Party, August 7, 1979

This resolution was submitted by the United Secretariat to the 1979 World Congress of the Fourth International. The vote of delegates and fraternal observers was: 100 for, 0.5 against, 6 abstentions, 6.5 not voting.

The basic Marxist positions on women's oppression are part of the programmatic foundations of the Fourth International. But this is the first full resolution on women's liberation adopted by the international. Its purpose is to set down our basic analysis of the character of women's oppression, and the place the struggle against that oppression occupies in our perspectives for all three sectors of the world revolution: the advanced capitalist countries, the colonial and semicolonial world, the workers states.

I. THE CHARACTER OF WOMEN'S OPPRESSION

The new rise of women's struggles

1. Since the late 1960s a growing revolt by women against their oppression as a sex has emerged. Throughout the world, millions of women, especially young women—students, working women, housewives—are beginning to challenge some of the most fundamental features of their centuries-old oppression.

The first country in which this radicalization of women appeared as a mass phenomenon was the United States. It was announced by the blossoming of thousands of women's liberation groups and in the mobilization of tens of thousands of women in the August 26, 1970, demonstrations commemorating the fiftieth anniversary of the victorious conclusion of the American women's suffrage struggle.

But the new wave of struggles by women in North America was not an exceptional and isolated development, as the emergence of the women's liberation movement throughout the advanced capitalist countries soon demonstrated.

The new women's liberation movement came on the historical scene as part of a more general upsurge of the working class and all exploited and oppressed sectors of the world population. This upsurge has taken many forms, from economic strikes, to struggles against national oppression, to student demonstrations, to demands for environmental protection, to an international movement against the imperialist war in Vietnam. Although the women's movement began among students and professional women, the demands it raised, combined with the growing contradictions within the capitalist system, began to mobilize much broader layers. It began to affect the consciousness, expectations, and actions of significant sections of the working class, male and female.

In many countries the new rise of women's struggles preceded any widespread changes in the combativity of organized labor. In others, such as Spain, it was intertwined with the explosive rise of struggles by the working class on every front. But in virtually every case, the movement rose outside of, and independent from, the existing mass organizations of the working class, which were then obliged to respond to this new phenomenon. The development of the women's movement has thus become an important factor in the political and ideological battle to weaken the hold of the bourgeoisie, and its agents within the working class.

The swift growth of the women's liberation movement, and the role it has played in the deepening class struggle, both internationally and in specific countries, confirm that the fight for women's liberation must be regarded as a fundamental component of the new rise of the world revolution.

2. This radicalization of women is unprecedented in the depth of the economic, social, and political ferment it expresses and in its implications for the struggle against capitalist oppression and exploitation.

In country after country, growing numbers of women are taking part in large-scale campaigns against reactionary abortion and contraception statutes, oppressive marriage laws, inadequate child-care facilities, and legal restrictions on equality. They are exposing and resisting the ways in which sexism is expressed in all spheres—from politics, employment, and education to the most intimate aspects of daily life, including the weight of domestic drudgery and the violence and intimidation that women are subjected to in the home and on the street.

Women are raising demands that challenge the specific forms their oppression takes under capitalism today, and are calling into question the deep-rooted traditional division of labor between men and women, from the home to the factory. More and more they are demanding affirmative action to open the doors previously closed to women in all arenas, and overcome the legacy of centuries of institutionalized discrimination.

They are insisting upon the right to participate with complete equality in all forms of social, economic and cultural activity—equal education, equal access to jobs, equal pay for equal work.

In order to make this equality possible, women are searching for ways to end their domestic servitude. They are demanding that women's household chores be socialized and no longer organized as "women's work." The most conscious recognize that society, as opposed to the individual family unit, should take responsibility for the young, the old, and the sick.

At the very center of the women's liberation movement has been the fight to decriminalize abortion and make it available to all women. The right to control their own bodies, to *choose* whether to bear children, when, and how many, is recognized by millions of women as an elementary precondition for their liberation.

Such demands go to the very heart of the specific oppression of women exercised through the family and strike at the pillars of class society. They indicate the degree to which the struggle for women's liberation is a fight to transform all human social relations and place them on a new and higher plane.

3. The fact that the women's liberation movement began to emerge as an international phenomenon even prior to the exacerbation of capitalism's worldwide economic contradictions in the mid-1970s only serves to underscore the deep roots of this rebellion. It is one of the clearest symptoms of the depth of the social crisis of the bourgeois order today.

These struggles illustrate the degree to which the outmoded capitalist relations and institutions generate deepening contradictions in every sector of society and precipitate new expressions of the class struggle. The death agony of capitalism brings new layers into direct conflict with the fundamental needs and prerogatives of the bourgeoisie, bringing forth new allies, and strengthening the working class in its struggle to overthrow the capitalist system. The development of the struggle by women against their oppression has already begun to deprive the ruling class of one of the principal weapons it has long used to divide and weaken the exploited and oppressed.

4. Women's oppression has been an essential feature of class society throughout the ages. But the practical tasks of uprooting its causes, as well as combating its effects, could not be posed on a mass scale before the era of the transition from capitalism to socialism. The fight for women's liberation is inseparable from the workers' struggle to abolish capitalism. It constitutes an integral part of the socialist revolution and the communist perspective of a classless society.

The replacement of the patriarchal family system rooted in private property by a superior organization of human relations is a prime objective of the socialist revolution. This process will accelerate and deepen as the material and ideological foundations of the new communist order are brought into being.

The development of the women's liberation movement today advances the class struggle, strengthens its forces, and enhances the prospects for socialism.

5. Women can achieve their liberation only

through the victory of the world socialist revolution. This goal can be realized only by mobilizing and organizing masses of women as a powerful component of the class struggle. Therein lies the objective revolutionary dynamic of the struggle for women's liberation and the fundamental reason why the Fourth International must concern itself with, and help to provide revolutionary leadership for, women struggling to achieve their liberation.

Origin and nature of women's oppression

1. The oppression of women is not determined by their biology, as many contend. Its origins are economic and social in character. Throughout the evolution of pre-class and class society, women's childbearing function has always been the same. But their social status has not always been that of a degraded domestic servant, subject to man's control and command.

2. Before the development of class society, during the historical period that Marxists have traditionally referred to as primitive communism (subsistence societies), social production was organized communally and its product shared equally. There was therefore no exploitation or oppression of one group or sex by another because no material basis for such social relations existed. Both sexes participated in social production, helping to assure the sustenance and survival of all. The social status of both women and men reflected the indispensable roles that each of them played in this productive process.

3. The origin of women's oppression is intertwined with the transition from pre-class to class society. The exact process by which this complex transition took place is a continuing subject of research and discussion even among those who subscribe to a materialist historical view. However, the fundamental lines along which women's oppression emerged are clear. The change in women's status developed along with the growing productivity of human labor based on agriculture, the domestication of animals, and stock raising; the rise of new divisions of labor, craftsmanship, and commerce; the private appropriation of an increasing social surplus; and the development of the possibility for some humans to prosper from the exploitation of the labor of others.

In these specific socioeconomic conditions, as the exploitation of human beings became profitable for a privileged few, women, because of their biological role in production, became valuable property. Like slaves and cattle, they were a source of wealth. They alone could produce new human beings whose labor power could be exploited. Thus the purchase of women by men, along with all rights to their future offspring, arose as one of the economic and social institutions of the new order based on private property. Women's primary social role was increasingly defined as domestic servant and child-bearer.

Along with the private accumulation of wealth, the patriarchal family developed as the institution by which responsibility for the unproductive members of society—especially the young—was transferred from society as a whole to an identifiable individual or small group of individuals. It was the primary socioeconomic institution for perpetuating from one generation to the next the class divisions of society—divisions between those who possessed property and lived off the wealth produced by the labor of others, and those who, owning no property, had to work for others to live. The destruction of the egalitarian and communal traditions and structures of primitive communism was essential for the rise of an exploiting class and its accelerated private accumulation of wealth.

This was the origin of the patriarchal family. In fact, the word family itself, which is still used in the Latin-based languages today, comes from the original Latin *famulus*, which means household slave, and *familia*, the totality of slaves belonging to one man.

Women ceased to have an independent place in social production. Their productive role was determined by the family to which they belonged, by the man to whom they were subordinate. This economic dependence determined the second-class social status of women, on which the cohesiveness and continuity of the patriarchal family has always depended. If women could simply take their children and leave, without suffering any economic or social hardship, the patriarchal family would not have survived through the millennia.

The patriarchal family and the subjugation of women thus came into existence along with the other institutions of emerging class society in order to buttress nascent class divisions and perpetuate the private accumulation of wealth. The state, with its police and armies, laws and courts, enforced this relationship. Ruling-class ideology, including religion, arose on this basis and played a vital role in justifying the degradation of the female sex.

Women, it was said, were physically and mentally inferior to men and therefore were "naturally" or biologically the second sex. While the subjugation of women has always had different consequences for women of distinct classes, all women regardless of class were and are oppressed as part of the female sex.

4. The family system is the fundamental institution of class society that determines and maintains the specific character of the oppression of the female sex.

Throughout the history of class society, the family system has proved its value as an institution of class rule. The form of the family has evolved and adapted itself to the changing needs of the ruling classes as the modes of production and forms of private property have gone through different stages of development. The family system under classical slavery was different from the family system during feudalism (there was no real slave family). Both were quite different from what is often called the urban "nuclear family" of today.

Moreover, the family system simultaneously fulfills different social and economic requirements in reference to classes with different productive roles and property rights whose interests are diametrically opposed. For example, the "family" of the serf and the "family" of the nobleman were quite different socioeconomic formations. However, they were both part of the family *system,* an institution of class rule that has played an indispensable role at each stage in the history of class society.

In class society the family is the only place most people can turn to try to satisfy some basic human needs, such as love and companionship. However poorly the family may meet these needs for many, there is no real alternative as long as private property exists. The disintegration of the family under capitalism brings with it much misery and suffering precisely because no superior framework for human relations can yet emerge.

But providing for affection and companionship is not what defines the nature of the family system. It is an economic and social institution whose functions can be summarized as follows:

a. The family is the basic mechanism through which the ruling classes abrogate social responsibility for the economic well-being of those whose labor power they exploit—the masses of humanity. The ruling class tries, to the degree possible, to force each family to be responsible for its own, thus institutionalizing the unequal distribution of income, status and wealth.

b. The family system provides the means for passing on property ownership from one generation to the next. It is the basic social mechanism for perpetuating the division of society into classes.

c. For the ruling class, the family system provides the most inexpensive and ideologically acceptable mechanism for reproducing human labor. Making the family responsible for care of the young means that the portion of society's accumulated wealth—appropriated as private property—that is utilized to assure reproduction of the laboring classes is minimized. Furthermore, the fact that each family is an atomized unit, fighting to assure the survival of its own, hinders the most exploited and oppressed from uniting in common action.

d. The family system enforces a social division of labor in which women are fundamentally defined by their childbearing role and assigned tasks immediately associated with this reproductive function: care of the other family members. Thus the family institution rests on and reinforces a social division of labor involving the domestic subjugation and economic dependence of women.

e. The family system is a repressive and conservatizing institution that reproduces within itself the hierarchical, authoritarian relationships necessary to the maintenance of class society as a whole. It fosters the possessive, competitive, and aggressive attitudes necessary to the perpetuation of class divisions.

It molds the behavior and character structure of children from infancy through adolescence. It trains, disciplines, and polices them, teaching submission to established authority. It then curbs rebellious, nonconformist impulses. It represses and distorts all sexuality, forcing it into socially acceptable channels of male and female sexual activity for reproductive purposes and socioeconomic roles. It inculcates all the social values and behavioral norms that individuals must acquire in order to survive in class society and submit to its domination. It distorts all human relationships by imposing on them the framework of economic compulsion, personal dependence, and sexual repression.

5. Under capitalism, as in previous historical epochs, the family has evolved. But the family system continues to be an indispensable institution of class rule, fulfilling all the economic and social functions outlined.

Among the bourgeoisie, the family provides for the transmission of private property from generation to generation. Marriages often assure profitable alliances or mergers of large blocs of capital, especially in the early stages of capital accumulation.

Among the classical petty bourgeoisie, such as farmers, craftsmen, or small shopkeepers, the family is also a unit of production based on the labor of family members.

For the working class, while the family provides some degree of mutual protection for its own members, in the most basic sense it is an alien class institution, one that is imposed on the working class, and serves the economic interests of the bourgeoisie not the workers. Yet working people are indoctrinated from childhood to regard it (like wage labor, private property and the state) as the most natural and imperishable of human relations.

a. With the rise of capitalism and the growth of the working class, the family unit among the workers ceases to be a petty-bourgeois unit of production although it remains the basic unit through which consumption and reproduction of labor power are organized. Each member of the family sells his or her labor power individually on the labor market. The basic economic bond that previously held together the family of the exploited and oppressed—i.e., the fact that they had to work together cooperatively in order to survive—begins to dissolve. As women are drawn into the labor market they achieve some degree of economic independence for the first time since the rise of class society. This begins to undermine the acceptance by women of their domestic subjugation. As a result, the family system is undermined.

b. Thus there is a contradiction between the increasing integration of women in the labor market and the survival of the family. As women achieve greater economic independence and more equality, the family institution begins to disintegrate. But the family system is an indispensable pillar of class rule. It must be preserved if capitalism is to survive.

c. The growing number of women in the labor market creates a deep contradiction for the capitalist class, especially during periods of accelerated expansion. They must employ more women to profit from their superexploitation. Yet the employment of women cuts across their ability to carry out the basic unpaid domestic labor of childrearing for which women are responsible. So the state must begin to buttress the family, helping to assure and subsidize some of the economic and social functions it used to fulfill, such as education, child care, etc.

But such social services are more costly than the unpaid domestic labor of women. They absorb some of the surplus value that would otherwise be appropriated by the owners of capital. They cut into profits. Moreover, social programs of this kind foster the idea that society, not the family, should be responsible for the welfare of its nonproductive members. They raise the social expectations of the working class.

d. Unpaid work by women in the home—cooking, cleaning, washing, caring for children—plays a specific role under capitalism. This household work is a necessary element in the reproduction of labor power sold to the capitalists (either a woman's own labor power, her husband's, or her children's, or that of any other member of the family).

Other things being equal, if women did not perform unpaid labor inside the families of the working class, the general wage level would have to rise. Real wages would have to be high enough to purchase the goods and services which are now produced within the family. (Of course, the general standard of living necessary for the reproduction of labor power is a historically determined given at any time in any country. It cannot be drastically reduced without a crushing defeat of the working class.) Any general decrease of unpaid domestic labor by women would thus cut into total profits, changing the proportion between profits and wages in favor of the proletariat.

However useful it may be, a woman's household work produces no commodities for the market and thus produces no value or surplus value. Nor does it directly enter into the process of capitalist exploitation. In value terms, unpaid domestic work in the family affects the *rate* of surplus value. Indirectly, it increases the total mass of social surplus value. This holds true whether such labor is performed by women, or shared by men.

It is the capitalist class, not men in general, and certainly not male wage earners, which profits from women's unpaid labor in the household. This "exploitation" of the family of the toilers, the burden of which falls overwhelmingly on women, can be eradicated only by overthrowing capitalism and socializing domestic chores in the process of socialist reconstruction.

e. The indispensable role of the family and the dilemma that the growing employment of women creates for the ruling class becomes clearest in periods of economic crisis. The rulers must accomplish two goals.

They must drive a significant number of women from the work force to reestablish the reserve labor pool and lower wage levels.

They must cut the growing costs of social services provided by the state and transfer the economic burden and responsibility for these services back onto the individual family of the worker.

In order to accomplish both of these objectives, they must launch an ideological offensive against the very concept of women's equality and independence, and reinforce the responsibility of the individual family for its own children, its elderly, its sick. They must reinforce the image of the family as the only "natural" form of human relations, and convince women who have begun to rebel against their subordinate status that true happiness comes only through fulfilling their "natural" and primary role as wife-mother-housekeeper. To their dismay, the capitalists are now discovering that despite appeals to austerity and dire warnings of crisis, the more thoroughly women are integrated into the work force, the more difficult it is to push sufficient numbers back into the home.

f. In the early stages of industrialization the unregulated, unbridled, brutal exploitation of women and children often goes so far as to seriously erode the family structure in the working class and threaten its usefulness as a system for organizing, controlling, and reproducing the work force.

This was the trend that Marx and Engels drew attention to in nineteenth-century England. They predicted the rapid disappearance of the family in the working class. They were correct in their basic insight and understanding of the role of the family in capitalist society, but they misestimated the latent capacity of capitalism to slow down the pace of development of its inherent contradictions. They underestimated the ability of the ruling class to step in to regulate the employment of women and children and shore up the family in order to preserve the capitalist system itself. Under strong pressure from the labor movement to ameliorate the brutal exploitation of women and children the state intervened in the long-term interests of the capitalist class—even though this cut across the aim of individual capitalists to squeeze every drop of blood out of each worker for sixteen hours a day and let them die at thirty.

g. Capitalist politicians responsible for shaping policies to protect and defend the interests of the ruling class are extremely conscious of the indispensable economic, social, and political role of the family and the need to maintain it as the basic social nucleus under capitalism. "Defense of the family" is not only some peculiar demagogic shibboleth of the ultraright. Maintenance of the family system is the basic political policy of every capitalist state, dictated by the social and economic needs of capitalism itself.

6. Under capitalism, the family system also provides the mechanism for the superexploitation of women as wage workers.

a. It provides capitalism with an exceptionally flexible reservoir of labor power that can be drawn into the labor force or sent back into the home with fewer social consequences than any other component of the reserve army of labor.

Because the entire ideological superstructure reinforces the fiction that women's place is in the home, high unemployment rates for women cause relatively less social protest. After all, it is said, women work only to supplement an already existing source of income for the family. When they are unemployed, they are occupied with their household chores, and are not so obviously "out of work." The anger and resentment they feel is often dissipated as a serious social threat by the general isolation and atomization of women in separate, individual households. Thus in any period of economic crisis, the austerity measures of the ruling class always include attacks on women's right to work, including increased pressure on women to accept part-time employment, cutbacks in unemployment benefits for "housewives," and the reduction of social services such as child-care facilities.

b. Because women's "natural" place is supposed to be in the home, capitalism has a widely accepted rationalization for perpetuating:

1) the employment of women in low-paying, unskilled jobs. "They aren't worth training because they'll only get pregnant or married and quit."

2) unequal pay rates and low pay. "They're only working to buy gadgets and luxuries anyway."

3) deep divisions within the working class itself. "She's taking a job a man should have."

4) the fact that women workers are not proportionally integrated in the trade unions and other organizations of the working class. "She shouldn't be running around going to meetings. She should be home taking care of the kids."

c. Since all wage structures are built from the bottom up, this superexploitation of women as a reserve work force plays an irreplaceable role in holding down men's wages as well.

d. The subjugation of women within the family system provides the economic, social, and ideological foundations that make their superexploitation possible. Women workers are exploited not only as wage labor but also as a pariah labor pool defined by sex.

7. Because the oppression of women is historically intertwined with the division of society into classes and with the role of the family as the basic unit of class society, this oppression can only be eradicated with the abolition of private ownership of the means of production. Today it is these class relations of production—not the productive capacities of humanity—which constitute the obstacle to transferring to society as a whole the social and economic functions borne under capitalism by the individual family.

8. The materialist analysis of the historical origin and economic roots of women's oppression is essential to developing a program and perspective capable of winning women's liberation. To reject this scientific explanation inevitably leads to one of two errors:

a. One error, made by many who claim to follow the Marxist method, is to deny, or at least downplay, the oppression of women as a sex throughout the entire history of class society. They see the oppression of women purely and simply as an aspect of the exploitation of the working class. This view gives weight and importance to struggles by women only in their capacity as wage workers on the job. It says women will be liberated, in passing, by the socialist revolution, so there is no special need for them to organize as women fighting for their own demands.

In rejecting the need for women to organize against their oppression, they only reinforce divisions within the working class, and retard the development of class consciousness among women who begin to rebel against their subordinate status.

b. A symmetrical error is made by those who argue that male domination of women existed before class society began to emerge. This was concretized, they hold, through a sexual division of labor. Thus, patriarchal oppression must be explained by reasons other than the development of private property and class society. They see patriarchy as a set of oppressive relations parallel to but independent of class relations.

Those who have developed this analysis in a systematic way usually isolate the fact of women's role in reproduction and concentrate on it alone. They largely ignore the primacy of cooperative labor, the essence of human society, and place little weight on women's place in the process of production at each historical stage. Some even go so far as to theorize a timeless patriarchal mode of reproduction with male control over the means of reproduction (women). They often put forward psychoanalytical explanations which readily fall into ahistorical idealism, rooting oppression in biological and/or psychological drives torn out of the materialist framework of social relations.

This current, sometimes organized as "radical feminists," contains both conscious anti-Marxists and others who consider themselves to be making a "feminist redefinition of Marxism." But the view that women's oppression is parallel to, not rooted in, the emergence and development of class exploitation leads the most consistent to pose the need for a political party of women based on a "feminist" program that pretends to be independent of the class struggle. They are hostile to and reject the need for women and men to organize together on the basis of a revolutionary working-class program to end both class exploitation and sexual oppression. They see little need for alliances in struggle with others who are oppressed and exploited.

Both of these one-sided approaches deny the revolutionary dynamic of the struggle for women's liberation as a form of the class struggle. Both fail to recognize that the struggle for women's liberation, to be successful, must go beyond the bounds of capitalist property relations. Both reject the implications this fact has for the working class and its revolutionary Marxist leadership.

Roots of the new radicalization of women

1. The women's liberation movement of today stands on the shoulders of the earlier struggles by women at the turn of the century.

With the consolidation of industrial capitalism throughout the nineteenth century, increasing numbers of women were integrated into the labor market. The gap between the social and legal status of women inherited from feudalism and their new economic status as wage workers selling their labor power in the market produced glaring contradictions. For women of the ruling class, too, capitalism opened the door to economic independence. Out of these contradictions arose the first wave of women's struggles aimed at winning full legal equality with men.

Among those fighting for women's rights were different political currents. Many of the suffragist leaders were women who believed the vote should be won by showing the ruling class that they were loyal defenders of the capitalist system. Some linked the suffragist struggle to support for imperialism in World War I and often opposed the right to vote for propertyless men and women, immigrants, Blacks.

But there was also a strong current of socialist women in a number of countries who saw the fight for women's rights as part of the working-class struggle and mobilized support from working-class women and men on that basis. They fought for the right to vote and played a decisive role in the suffrage struggle in countries like the United States. They also raised and fought for other demands such as equal pay and contraception services.

Even some of the semicolonial countries such as Chile, Argentina, and Mexico saw the emergence of feminist groups during this same period.

Through struggle the women of the most advanced capitalist countries won, to varying degrees, several important democratic rights: the right to higher education, the right to engage in trades and professions, the right to receive and dispose of their own wages (which had been considered the right of the husband or father), the right to own property, the right to divorce, the right to participate in political organizations. In several countries this first upsurge culminated in mass struggles for the right to vote.

2. Women's suffrage, following or sometimes accompanying universal male suffrage, was an important objective gain for the working class. It reflected, and in turn helped advance, the changing social status of women. For the first time in class society, women were legally considered citizens fit to participate in public affairs, with the right to a voice on major political questions, not just private household matters.

Even though the underlying cause of the subordinate status of women lies in the very foundations of class society itself and women's special role within the family, not in the formal denial of equality under the law, the extension of democratic rights to women gave them greater latitude for action and helped later generations see that the sources of women's oppression lay deeper.

3. The roots of the new radicalization of women are to be found in the economic and social changes of the post–World War II years, which have effected deepening contradictions in the capitalist economy, in the status of women, and in the patriarchal family system. To varying degrees the same factors were at work in every country that remained within the world capitalist market. But it is not surprising that the resurgence of the women's movement today first came about in the most advanced capitalist countries—such as the United States, Canada, and Britain—where these changes and contradictions had developed the furthest.

a. Advances in medical science and technology in the field of birth control and abortion have created the means by which masses of women can have greater control over their reproductive functions. Control by women over their own bodies is a precondition for women's liberation.

While such medical techniques are more widely available, reactionary laws, reinforced by bourgeois customs, religious bigotry, and the entire ideological superstructure of class society, often stand in the way of women exercising control over their own reproductive functions. Financial, legal, psychological, and "moral" barriers are fabricated to try to prevent women from demanding the right to choose whether and when to bear children. In addition, the limits placed on research due to capitalist profit considerations and sexist disregard for the lives of women have meant continuing health hazards for women using the most convenient methods of birth control.

This contradiction between what is possible and what actually exists affects the lives of all women. It has given rise to the powerful abortion rights struggles, which have been at the center of the women's movement on an international scale.

b. The prolonged boom conditions of the postwar expansion significantly increased the percentage of women in the labor force.

To take the United States as an example, in 1950, 33.9 percent of all women 18 to 64 years of age were in the labor force. By 1975 this had risen to 54 percent. Between 1960 and 1975, nearly two-thirds of all new jobs created were taken by women. Working women accounted for 29.1 percent of the total labor force in 1950; 43 percent by 1978.

Equally important, the percentage of working women with children increased dramatically, as did the percentage of working women who were heads of households.

In Spain, three times as many women are working today as in 1930.

In Britain, between 1881 and 1951 the proportion of women in employment was fairly stable, remaining at about 25 to 27 percent. By 1965, 34 percent of all women between 16 and 64 were in full-time employment, 17.9 percent were in part-time employment, and a total of 54.3 percent came within the category of "economically active." Nearly two-thirds of the working women were married.

Only some countries that still had a high percentage of agricultural workers after the Second World War have experienced a decline in female employment over the postwar period. This was due to the fact that with the migration to the cities, many women were not reintegrated into the so-called active population. In Italy, for example, where this factor was combined with the development of massive unemployment in small enterprises of the "typically female" sector, there has been a decline in the female percentage of the work force.

In extremely depressed regions such as southern Italy and northern Portugal, this retrogression has actually been coupled with the resurgence of cottage industry on a significant scale. Women are induced to do piecework on their sewing machines at home, thus saving the bosses the costs of factory maintenance, health and social security payments, strikes and other "problems" caused by an organized work force.

As the influx of women into the labor force has taken place, there has been no substantial change in the degree of wage discrimination against women. In many countries this differential between the sexes has actually widened.

This is primarily because the increased employment of women has not been spread evenly over all job categories. In nearly all countries women represent from 70 to 90 percent of the work force employed in textiles, shoes, ready-to-wear clothing, tobacco, and other light industry—that is, sectors in which wages are lowest. Women also account for 70 percent or more of people employed in the service sector, with the greatest majority of women occupying the least remunerative positions: secretaries, file clerks, health workers, teachers in primary schools, keypunch operators.

Discrimination in sectors of employment—exacerbated by unequal pay for the same work in many cases—is the fundamental reason why, even in those countries where the labor movement has fought the hardest on this question, the average wage for women barely exceeds 75 percent of the average wage for men. This also explains why the differential may even widen with the massive entry of women into the lowest-paid sectors of the economy. This is the case in the United States, where the median income of full-time, year-round women workers was 64 percent of that of men in 1955 but dropped to 59 percent in 1977.

Despite their growing place in the work force, women are still forced to assume the majority, if not the totality, of domestic tasks in addition to their wage labor. As a consequence, they often quit working temporarily when they have children, especially when they are faced with many hours of forced overtime, and then have difficulty finding new jobs later. If they continue to work they are obliged to stay home when a child is sick.

This has led to a significant increase in part-time work by women—either because they cannot find full-time employment, or because they cannot otherwise cope with their domestic chores. But part-time work invariably brings with it lower wages, less job security, few social security benefits, and less likelihood of unionization.

The growing weight of women in the work force has had a strong impact on the attitudes of their male fellow workers. This is especially true where women have begun to fight their way into jobs in basic industry from which women were previously excluded.

But women workers still face many forms of discrimination and sexist abuse, promoted, organized and maintained by the bosses. Their fellow workers are often not aware of them, and sometimes express the same backward attitudes. And the labor bureaucracy blocks the use of union power to overcome the special obstacles women face—such as the refusal to give paid time off for maternity leaves, health hazards that are doubly dangerous for pregnant women, and harassment by foremen and supervisors who use their control over jobs to try to pressure women into sexual relations.

c. The rise in the average educational level of women has further heightened the contradictions. As labor productivity increases and the general cultural level of the working class rises, more women finish their years of secondary education. Women are also accepted into institutions of higher education on a qualitatively larger scale than ever before.

Yet, as the employment statistics indicate, the percentage of women holding jobs commensurate with their educational level has not kept pace. In all areas of the job market, from industry to the professions, women with higher educational qualifications are usually bypassed by men with less education. Moreover, throughout primary and secondary school, girls continue to be pushed—through required courses of study or through more indirect pressures—into what are considered women's jobs and roles.

As they receive more education and as social struggles raise their individual expectations, the stifling and mind-deadening drudgery of household chores and the constrictions of family life become increasingly unbearable. Thus the heightened educational level of women, combined with an intensification of the class struggle, has deepened the contradiction between women's demonstrated abilities and broadened aspirations, and their actual social and economic status.

d. The functions of the family unit in advanced capitalist society have continually contracted. It has become less and less a unit of petty production—either agricultural or domestic (canning, weaving, sewing, baking, etc.). The urban nuclear family of today has come a long way from the productive farm family of previous centuries. At the same time, in their search for profits, consumer-oriented capitalist industry and advertising seek to maximize the atomization and duplication of domestic work in order to sell each household its own washer, dryer, dishwasher, vacuum cleaner, etc.

As the standard of living rises, the average number of children per family declines sharply. Industrially prepared foods and other conveniences become increasingly available. Yet, in spite of the technological advances, surveys in a number of imperialist countries have shown that women who have more than one child and a full-time job must put in 80 to 100 hours of work per week—more hours than similar surveys conducted in 1926 and 1952 revealed. While appliances have eased certain domestic tasks, the shrinking size of the average family unit has meant that women are less able to call on grandparents, aunts, or sisters to help.

With all these changes, the objective basis for confining women to the home becomes less and less compelling. Yet the needs of the ruling class dictate that the family system be preserved. Bourgeois ideology and social conditioning continue to reinforce the reactionary fiction that a woman's identity and fulfillment must come from her role as wife-mother-housekeeper. The contradiction between reality and myth becomes increasingly obvious and intolerable to growing numbers of women.

This state of affairs is frequently referred to as "the crisis of the family," which is expressed in the soaring divorce rates, increased numbers of runaway children and rising domestic violence.

4. Greater democratic rights and broader social opportunities have not "satisfied" women, or inclined them to a passive acceptance of their inferior social status and economic dependence. On the contrary, they have stimulated new struggles and more far-reaching demands.

It was generally the young, college-educated women, those who enjoyed a relatively greater freedom of choice, and those most affected by the youth radicalization of the 1960s, who first articulated the grievances of women in an organized and outspoken way. This led some who consider themselves Marxists to conclude that women's liberation is basically a middle-class or bourgeois protest movement that has no serious interest for revolutionists or the masses of working-class women. They could not be more wrong.

The initial development of the women's liberation movement served only to emphasize the depth and scope of women's oppression. Even those with many advantages in terms of education and other opportunities were and continue to be propelled into action. The most oppressed and exploited are not necessarily the first to articulate their discontent.

5. Contributing to the growth of the women's liberation movement in recent years, and increasing the involvement of working-class women, has been the drive to cut back social expenditures in most advanced capitalist countries. After the Second World War, in a context of heightened demands by the working class that more social services be provided by the state, the bourgeoisie, especially in Europe, was forced to expand housing developments, health services, and family allowance programs. Later, as the boom of the 1950s and 1960s generated a growing need for female labor power, facilities such as child-care centers and laundromats were extended in order to encourage women to seek employment.

South African women protest racist internal passport system.

Today, faced with deepening economic problems, the ruling class is slashing social expenditures and trying to shift the burden back onto the individual family, with all the consequences that has for women. But resistance to being driven out of their newly acquired places in the work force, and broad female opposition to social cutbacks such as the closing of child-care centers, have created unexpectedly thorny problems for the rulers in many countries. Imbued with a growing feminist consciousness, women have been more combative and less willing than ever before to shoulder a disproportionate burden in the current economic crisis.

6. While the women's radicalization has an independent dynamic of its own, determined by the specific character of women's oppression and the objective changes that have been described, it is not isolated from the more general upsurge of the class struggle taking place today. It is not directly dependent on other social forces, subordinate to their leadership, or beholden to their initiative. At the same time, the women's movement has been and remains deeply interconnected with the rise of other social struggles, all of which have likewise affected the consciousness of the entire working class.

a. From the beginning, the new upsurge of women's struggles has been strongly affected by the international youth radicalization and the increased challenge to bourgeois values and institutions that accompanied it. Young people—both male and female—began to question religion; to reject patriotism; to challenge authoritarian hierarchies from family, to school, to factory, to army; to reject the inevitability of a lifetime of alienated labor. Radicalized youth began to rebel against sexual repression and to challenge the traditional morality equating sex with reproduction. For women, this involved a challenge to the time-honored education of females to be sexually passive, sentimental, fearful, and timid. Masses of youth, including young women, became more conscious of their sexual misery and tried to search for more fulfilling types of personal relationships.

b. One of the factors contributing to the international youth radicalization has been the role played by the liberation struggles of oppressed nations and nationalities, both in the colonial world and in the advanced capitalist countries. Moreover, these have had a powerful impact on the consciousness concerning women's oppression in general. For example, the Black struggle in the United States played a crucial role in bringing about a widespread awareness and rejection of racist stereotypes. The obvious similarities between racist attitudes and sexist stereotypes of women as inferior, emotional, dependent, dumb-but-happy creatures produced an increasing sensitivity to and rejection of such caricatures.

As the feminist movement has developed in the advanced capitalist countries, women of the oppressed nationalities have begun to play an increasingly prominent role. As oppressed nationalities, as women, and frequently as superexploited workers, these women suffer a double and often triple oppression. Their objective place in society means they are in a position to play a strategically important role in the working class and among its allies.

But there has generally been a lag in the pace with which women of oppressed nationalities have become conscious of their specific oppression as women. There are several reasons for this. For many, the depth of their national oppression initially overshadows their oppression as women. Many radical nationalist movements have refused to take up the demands of women, calling them divisive to the struggle for national liberation. The organized women's movement has often failed in its obligation to address itself to the needs of the most oppressed and exploited layers of women and understand the special difficulties they face. In addition, the hold of the family is often particularly strong among women of the oppressed nationalities, since the family sometimes seems to provide a partial buffer against the devastating pressures of racism and cultural annihilation.

Nevertheless, once the radicalization begins, experience has already shown it takes on an explosive character, propelling women of oppressed nationalities into the leadership of many social and political struggles, including struggles on the job, in the unions, on campuses and in the communities, as well as the feminist movement. They rapidly come to understand that the struggle against their oppression as women does not weaken but strengthens the struggle against their national oppression.

c. Contributing to the rise of the women's movement has been the crisis of the traditional organized religions, especially the Catholic church. The weakening hold of the church (accompanied by a growth in occultism and mysticism) is a dramatic manifestation of the ideological crisis of bourgeois society. All organized religion, which is part of the superstructure of class society, is predicated on and reinforces the notion that women are inferior, if not the very incarnation of evil and animality. Christianity and Judaism, which mark the cultures of the advanced capitalist countries, have always upheld the inequality of women and denied them the right to separate sexuality from reproduction.

In countries where the Catholic church has had a particularly strong hold, it is often radicalizing women who are spearheading the challenge to the power and ideological hold of the church, as shown in the demonstrations of tens of thousands for the right to abortion in Italy, or the demonstrations in 1976 against the anti-adultery laws in Spain.

In Israel, too, the fight for abortion rights shook the stability of the Begin government.

In many oppressed nations such as Quebec, Ireland, and Euzkadi (the Basque country), and among the Chicano people, the repressive ideology of the Catholic church has combined in a particularly oppressive way with the myth of the "woman-mother," the center of the family, as the only pole of social, emotional, and political stability, the only refuge from the ravages of national oppression. In Quebec for years this amalgam was expressed in the concept of the "revenge of the cradle," suggesting the Quebecois women must save the nation from assimilation by having many children.

d. The lesbian-feminist movement emerged as an interrelated but distinct aspect of the radicalization of women.

Lesbians have organized as a component of the gay rights movement, generally finding it necessary to fight within the gay movement for their specific demands as gay *women* to be recognized. But lesbians are also oppressed as women. Many radicalized as women first and felt the discrimination they suffered because of their sexual orientation was only one element of the social and economic limitations women face in trying to determine the course of their lives. Thus many lesbians were in the forefront of the feminist movement from the very beginning. They have been part of every political current within the women's liberation movement, from lesbian-separatists to revolutionary Marxists, and they have helped to make the entire movement more conscious of the specific ways in which gay women are oppressed.

Because of the lesbian movement's insistence on the right of women to live independent of men, they often become the special target of attacks by reaction. From hate propaganda to violent physical assaults, the attacks on lesbians and the lesbian movement are really aimed against the women's movement as a whole. Attempts to divide the women's movement by lesbian-baiting must be rejected in a clear and uncompromising way if the struggle for women's liberation is to move forward.

e. In many of the advanced capitalist countries immigrant women workers have also played a special role. Not only are they superexploited as part of the work force. They are the victims of special discriminatory laws. As women, they often have no right to accompany their husbands to any given country unless they have been able to secure employment for themselves prior to immigrating. If they find work, they are often obliged to give it up to follow their husbands elsewhere. Government measures adopted in recent years to reduce the number of immigrant workers in many advanced capitalist countries have made these laws even more discriminatory.

In a country like Switzerland, where immigrant workers make up nearly 30 percent of the industrial work force, and in other European countries where immigrant women are a majority in some sectors such as the hospitals, immigrant women workers have played a decisive role in raising the political consciousness of the women's movement. They have helped lead struggles in industries that employ predominantly female workers. Even more importantly, they have helped stimulate discussion in the women's movement concerning the economic and social policies of the ruling class. Discriminatory laws in relationship to immigration in general; xenophobia and racism; the resulting divisions within the working class; the ways in which immigrant women are particularly affected by these divisions; the need for the trade unions and the women's movement to fight for the interests of the most superexploited layers; the problems faced by women who are isolated both in their own homes and by the hostile environment in which they live—all these are questions posed before the women's movement, helping to raise some of the most important aspects of a class-struggle perspective.

7. The fading of the postwar boom and the deepening economic, social, and political problems of imperialism on a world scale, highlighted by the 1974–75 international recession, led to an intensification of the attacks on women's rights on all levels. This did not lead to a decline in women's struggles, or relegate them to the sidelines as more powerful social forces came to the fore. Far from diminishing as the struggles of the organized working class sharpened in recent years, feminist consciousness and struggles by women continue to spread and to become more deeply intertwined with the developing social consciousness and political combativity of working-class women and men. Women's resistance to the economic, political, and ideological offensive of the ruling class has been stiffened by the heightened feminist awareness. Their struggles have been a powerful motor force of social protest and political radicalization.

Responses from the bourgeoisie and from currents in the workers movement

1. Divisions rapidly appeared inside the capitalist class over how best to respond to the new rise of women's struggles in order to blunt their impact and deflect their radical thrust. After initial attempts to dismiss the women's movement with ridicule and scorn, however, the prevailing view within the ruling class has been to give lip service to the idea that women have at least some just grievances. There has been an attempt to appear concerned—by setting up some special government departments, commissions, or projects to catch women's attention, while working assiduously to integrate the leadership of the women's movement into the accepted patterns of class collaboration. In most countries, the ruling class was forced to make a few concessions that seemed least harmful economically and ideologically—and then steadily tried to take them back.

In each case the aim has been the same, whatever the tactics: to contain the nascent radicalization within the framework of minimal reforms of the capitalist system.

In many European countries, there have been moves to liberalize maternity benefits by extending leaves, raising the percentage of pay women receive while on leave, or by guaranteeing work after a maternity leave without pay. In other countries, governments have ostentatiously debated the justice of promises for equal pay laws, or liberalized divorce laws. In the United States both capitalist political parties have gone on record for passage of an equal rights amendment to the constitution while in practice they sabotage each attempt to muster enough votes to make it law.

But when it comes to social programs that would have immediate and significant economic impact—such as the expansion of child-care facilities—the gains have been virtually nonexistent.

The most serious gain extracted by the international women's movement in the decade since it arose has been the significant expansion of access to legal abortion. In more than twenty countries there has been a marked liberalization of abortion laws.

In every country where women have made measurable progress toward establishing abortion as a right, it has rapidly become clear that this right is never secure under capitalism. Wherever women begin to fight for the right to control their own reproductive functions, the most reactionary defenders of the capitalist system have immediately mobilized to prevent that elementary precondition of women's liberation from being established. The right to choose is too great a challenge to the ideological underpinnings of women's oppression.

However, it is politically important to see clearly that far-right organizations such as "Laissez les vivre," "Oui à la vie," "Right to Life," and "Society for the Protection of the Unborn Child," which are linked to xenophobic, clerical, racist, or outright fascist currents, are nourished by official governmental policies. They function as fanatical protectors of the status quo, attempting to appeal to and mobilize the most backward prejudices that run deep in the working class and petty bourgeoisie, and they render a valuable service to the rulers. But without the backhanded—and sometimes open—encouragement of the dominant sectors of the ruling class, their role would be far less influential.

2. The emergence of the women's liberation movement has posed a profound challenge to all political currents claiming to represent the interests of the working class.

The Stalinists and Social Democrats especially were taken aback by the rapid development of a significant radicalization that did not look to them for leadership.

The responses given by the two mass reformist currents in the working class varied from one country to another depending on numerical strength, base in the working class and in the trade-union bureaucracies, and proximity to responsibility for the government of their own capitalist state. But in every case the reflexes of both Stalinists and Social Democrats have been determined by two sometimes conflicting objectives: their commitment to the basic institutions of class rule, including the family; and their need to maintain or strengthen their influence in the working class if they are to contain working-class struggles within the bounds of capitalist property relations.

The rise of the women's liberation movement forced both the Stalinists and Social Democrats to adapt to the changing political situation. The year 1975 in particular gave rise to a flurry of position-taking, partly in response to the initiatives of the bourgeoisie in the context of International Women's Year.

3. Under pressure from part of their own rank and file, Social Democratic parties have generally responded to the rise of the feminist movement more rapidly than the Communist parties. Even though the SPs officially have been reluctant to recognize the existence of the independent women's movement, individual women members of the SPs have often participated actively in the new organizations that have emerged.

The formal positions taken by the SPs have frequently been more progressive than those of the Stalinist parties, especially in regard to abortion as a woman's right. Wherever Socialist parties have had the opportunity to polish up their image at low cost by coming out in favor of liberalized abortion laws, they have not hesitated to do so. Kreisky in Austria and Brandt in Germany initially took such a tack. Faced with a growing women's movement in Australia, the Australian Labor Party attempted to win political support by granting subsidies to numerous small projects initiated by the movement, such as women's health centers and refuges. While these moves cost the Social Democrats little in economic terms, they served to temporarily draw the attention of women away from the inadequacy of their overall policies (on abortion and child care, for example) and helped the ALP to project itself as a "pro-woman" government.

But when confronted with the first signs of reaction from sectors of the bourgeoisie, the Social Democratic parties have been quick to retreat.

While the Labour Party in Britain was on record in favor of the right to abortion on request, the party remained silent about the reactionary proposals before parliament aimed at rolling back abortion rights to their pre-1967 status. Initially introduced in 1975 by a Labour MP, the new proposals would restrict the period of time in which women are permitted to obtain abortions, limit access to abortions for immigrant women, and inflict stiff penalties for all violations of the law.

Only in 1977, after a massive campaign by the independent women's movement, organized through the National Abortion Campaign (NAC), and under the pressure of its own ranks, did the Labour Party conference adopt a resolution defending the 1967 law.

The Social Democrats have proved especially useful to the bosses when it comes to imposing austerity measures to reduce the standard of living of the working class. While loudly protesting their commitment to easing the burdens of working-class women, Social Democratic governments have not hesitated to make the cuts in social services demanded by the bourgeoisie. In Denmark they eliminated 5,000 child-care workers from the state payroll with one stroke of the pen.

4. From the 1930s on, after the Stalinist bureaucracy consolidated its control of the USSR and transformed the parties of the Third International into apologists for the counterrevolutionary policies of the Kremlin, defense of the family as the ideal framework of human relations has been the line of Stalinist parties throughout the world. This not only served the needs of the bureaucratic caste in the Soviet Union itself but coincided with the need to defend the capitalist status quo elsewhere. The openly reactionary theories of the French CP on the family were first expounded when the new

family code was introduced in the USSR in 1934 and abortions were prohibited in 1936.

However demagogic they may be at times concerning women's double day of work, the demands raised by the CP today are most often proposals to rearrange things so women have an easier time meeting the tasks that fall on them in the home. From better maternity leaves, to shorter hours, to improved working conditions for women, the fight is often justified by the need to free women *for* their household chores—rather than *from* them by socializing the domestic burdens women bear. The other solution, which they sometimes propose, is to demand that men share the work load more equitably at home.

But the rise of the women's movement, the attempts of the bourgeoisie to capitalize on it, the responses of other currents in the workers movement, and the pressure of their own ranks have all compelled the Communist parties to modify and adjust their line. Even the most hidebound and rigid followers of the Kremlin, like the American Communist Party, have finally been forced to abandon some of their most reactionary positions such as opposition to an equal rights amendment to the constitution.

The deeper the radicalization, the more adroitly the CPs have had to maneuver by throwing themselves into the movement and adopting more radical verbiage.

The CPs have let women members engage in public discussion and develop scathing condemnations of capitalism's responsibilities for the miserable status of women. But when it comes to program and action, the CP's opposition to women's liberation duplicates their opposition to a class struggle fight for other needs of the working class. They are ready to shelve any demand or derail any struggle in the interests of consolidating or preserving whatever class-collaborationist alliance they are working for. Thus, despite the Italian CP's formal shift and decision to support liberalization of abortion laws, in 1976 the CP parliamentary deputies made a bloc with the Christian Democrats to kill abortion law reform because it was an obstacle to advancing toward the "historic compromise."

Moreover, there is often a conflict between the positions taken by the CP locally—where they sometimes express support for struggles to establish child-care centers or abortion-contraception clinics—and the actions of the CP nationally—where they support austerity measures to cut back on such social programs.

The discrepancy between the formal positions of the Communist parties and their betrayals in the class struggle, have already brought about some sharp tensions within those parties and in the trade unions they dominate. This is especially true because the absence of internal democracy deepens the frustrations of many women who begin to see the contradictions between their own personal commitment to women's liberation and the line of their party. They have no way to influence the positions of their organization. Thus, when the Spanish CP signed the class-collaborationist Moncloa pact, women formed an opposition group in the Madrid CP to fight for internal democracy.

In France, when opposition groupings began to form in the CP in 1978, women members of the party organized around the magazine *Elles Voient Rouge* (They See Red). They sought to defend their positions and fight the sectarian policies of the party which rejected united front action with other political groups on the abortion question or any other issue.

Organizationally, too, the Stalinists have been forced to adjust. In a number of countries the Stalinists formed their own women's organizations after the Second World War. Faced with the new radicalization of women, they have invariably tried to pass these organizations off in the eyes of the working class as the only real women's movement. The independent movement threatens their pretense of being the party that speaks for working-class women, and their initial reaction has been to deepen their sectarian stance.

In Spain, for example, the CP-controlled MDM (Movimiento Democrático de la Mujer—Democratic Movement of Women) declared that it alone *was* the women's movement, and the CP proclaimed itself to be the party of women's liberation. But despite the strength of the CP, the MDM was unable to dominate the radicalization of women, which was expressed through the flourishing of women's groups on all levels throughout the Spanish state. Unable to establish the MDM by fiat, the CP was forced to recognize the existence of other groups and work with them.

5. Involvement in the women's movement has brought similar contradictions for the Social Democratic parties as well. But at the same time, the ability of both the Stalinists and Social Democrats to adapt to some of the issues raised by radicalizing women has enhanced their ability to influence the general course of the movement. When these parties decide to support one or another mass mobilization, as they have in a number of countries recently on the abortion question, their reformist positions have all the more impact on large numbers of women. It would be a mistake to underestimate their political weight.

6. The Maoists and centrist organizations have most often adopted sectarian, economist positions on the women's liberation movement, considering it to be petty bourgeois and in conflict with their concept of the workers movement. Among these organizations, however, there have been basically two types of response. Some have refused to participate in the independent organizations and activities of the women's liberation movement. Many of these sectarian groups have set up their own auxiliary women's groups, which they counterpose to the living women's movement, arguing that such a course is the only genuinely communist strategy.

Other Maoist and centrist groups have oriented toward participating in the women's movement. But they have no understanding of the relationship between the class struggle and the fight for women's liberation. They reject a policy of united front action, and simply tail-end the women's movement. This was an important factor contributing to the crises that tore many such groups apart at the end of the 1970s.

7. The trade-union movement has also felt the impact of the radicalization of women and its bureaucracies have been obliged to respond to the pressures from women inside and outside the organized labor movement.

Like the Stalinists and Social Democrats, even in the best of cases labor officials try to limit union responsibility for women's demands to economic questions, such as equal pay or maternity leaves. As long as possible, they resist involving labor in fighting for issues such as abortion. However, the mass character of the unions, the growing number of women in their ranks, many of whom are increasingly active in women's commissions, makes such a stance by the union bureaucracies more difficult. This was clearly seen in October 1979 when the British Trades Union Congress, under growing pressure from its own ranks, called for a national demonstration in defense of abortion rights. Some 50,000 men and women turned out. Questions such as child care and the socialization of domestic work, conditions for part-time workers, and affirmative action programs for women are raised with greater frequency today in the union movement. In some cases women are explicitly posing these demands in the general framework of the need to break down the traditional division of labor between men and women.

By forcing these issues, women workers are calling into question the reformists' attempts to maintain a division between economic and political issues and otherwise limit whatever struggles develop. They are helping the working class to think in broad social terms and encouraging the ranks of the unions to turn to and use their basic class organizations to fight for all their needs.

As women try to win the union ranks and leadership to support their demands, they are obliged to take up the question of union democracy as well. They have to fight for the right to express themselves freely, to organize their own commissions or caucuses, to be represented in the union leaderships, and for the union to provide the kinds of facilities, such as child care during meetings, that will permit women to be fully active in the workers organizations.

Some unions have put out special literature, reactivated moribund women's commissions, organized meetings of women unionists, or established special training courses for women union leaders. In a number of countries special inter-union committees of women have been organized by the trade-union leadership on national, regional, or local levels. Elsewhere committees have been created under the impetus of the rank and file. The radicalization of women and the deepening economic crisis have also led to an increase in the rate of unionization of women workers in some advanced capitalist countries.

By and large, the creation of women's commissions within the unions has occurred with the blessing of the union bureaucracies. They hope to contain the radicalization of women in the unions and direct their energies in a way that will not threaten the comfortable status quo on any level—from the male monopoly of union leadership posts to the understanding between the bureaucracy and the bosses that the particular needs of women workers be ignored.

But this development reflects the huge impact that the women's liberation movement has already had on the organized labor movement. Such women's commissions within the unions are today more and more products of the women's movement as well as part of the labor movement. They stand at the intersection of the two and, if properly led, can help show the way forward for both.

Women's liberation in the colonial and semicolonial world

1. Women's liberation is not a matter of interest only to women of the advanced capitalist countries with their relatively high educational level and standard of living. On the contrary, it is of vital concern and importance to the masses of women throughout the world. The colonial and semicolonial countries are no exception.

There is great diversity in the economic and social conditions and cultural traditions in the colonial and semicolonial countries. They range from extremely primitive conditions in some areas to considerable industrialization in countries such as Puerto Rico and Argentina. All semicolonial and colonial countries, however, are defined by the imperialist domination they suffer in common. This also has specific effects on women in these countries.

Imperialist domination has meant that capitalist relations of production have been superimposed on, and have combined with, archaic, precapitalist modes of production and social relations, transforming them and incorporating them into the capitalist economy. In Western Europe the rise of capitalism was punctuated by bourgeois-democratic revolutions in the more advanced countries which broke the economic and political power of the old feudal ruling classes. But in the colonial countries imperialist penetration most often reinforced the privileges, hierarchies, and reactionary traditions of the precapitalist ruling classes, which it utilized wherever possible to maintain stability and maximize imperialist exploitation.

Using torture, extermination, rape, and other forms of terror on a mass scale, and in Africa through the outright enslavement of the native peoples, expanding European capitalism brutally colonized Latin America and parts of Asia and Africa and thrust them into the world market. With the European and eventually American conquerors came Christianity as well, which was often turned to advantage as one of the central links in the chain of subjugation.

For women in the semicolonial and colonial world the penetration of the capitalist market economy has a contradictory impact: on the one hand it introduces new economic relations that begin to lay the basis for women to overcome their centuries-old oppression. But on the other hand, it takes over and utilizes the archaic traditions, religious codes, and antiwoman prejudices, initially reinforcing them through new forms of discrimination and superexploitation.

In general, the situation of women is directly related to the degree of industrialization that has been achieved. But uneven and combined development in some societies can produce startling contradictions, such as relative economic independence for women who dominate very primitive agriculture in some areas of Africa.

2. In the colonial countries, the development of capitalist production proceeds according to the needs of imperialism. For this reason, industrialization takes place only slowly and in an unbalanced, distorted way, if at all. In most semicolonial countries, the majority of the population still lives on the land and is engaged in subsistence farming, utilizing extremely backward methods. The family—which generally includes various aunts, uncles, nieces, nephews, and grandparents—is the basic unit of petty agricultural production.

Women play a decisive economic role. Not only do they work long hours in the fields and home, but they produce children to share the burden of work and provide economic security in old age. They marry at puberty and often give birth to as many children as physically possible. Their worth is generally determined by the number of children they produce. A barren woman is considered a social disgrace and an economic disaster. Infertility is often grounds for divorce.

Because of its productive role, the hold of the family on all its members, but specifically on women, is strong. Combined with a primitive level of economic development, this brings about extreme deprivation and degradation for peasant women in the rural areas. In practice, they scarcely have any legal or social rights as individuals, and are often barely considered human. They live under virtually total domination and control by male members of their family. In many cases the restricted resources of the family unit are allocated first of all to the male members of the family; it is not uncommon for female children to receive less food and care, leading to stunted growth or early death from malnutrition. Female infanticide, both direct and through deliberate neglect, is still practiced in many areas. Often illiteracy rates for women approach 100 percent.

3. The incorporation of the colonial and semicolonial countries into the world capitalist market inevitably has an impact on the rural areas, however. Inflation and the inability to compete with larger units utilizing more productive methods lead to continuous waves of migration from the countryside to the cities. Often this migration begins with the males of the family, leaving the women, children, and elderly with an even heavier burden as they try to eke out an impoverished existence from the land on their own.

The desperate search for a job eventually leads millions of workers to leave their country of birth and migrate to the advanced industrial countries, where if they are lucky enough to find a job, it will be under miserable conditions of superexploitation.

The isolation and backward traditions of the rural areas tend to be challenged and broken down not only by migration to and from the cities but also by the diffusion of the mass media, such as radio and television.

4. With migration to the cities, the new conditions of life and labor begin to challenge the traditional norms and myths about the role of women.

In the cities the petty-bourgeois family as a productive unit rapidly disappears for most. Each family member is obliged to sell his or her labor power on the market as an individual. However, due to the extremely precarious employment situation, and the financial responsibilities that the semiproletarian city dwellers often have vis-à-vis their rural relatives, the immediate family often still includes aunts, uncles, cousins, brothers and sisters and their children, besides father, mother, and children.

Among the urban middle class and the more stable sectors of the proletariat, however, the family unit begins to become more restricted.

As they migrate to the cities, women have greater opportunity for education, for broader social contact, and for economic independence. The needs of capitalism, which bring increasing numbers of women out of family isolation, come into conflict with the old ideas about the role of women in society. In taking jobs as industrial or service workers, women begin to occupy positions that were previously forbidden them by backward prejudices and traditions. Those able to secure an education that permits them to break into professions, such as teaching and nursing, also serve as examples that contradict traditional attitudes, even in the eyes of those women who don't work. The myth of women's inferiority is increasingly called into question by this reality, which challenges their time-honored subordination.

Even for women who are not able to get an education or to work outside the home, city conditions help provide the possibility of escaping the mental prison that the rural family's isolation imposes on them. This happens through the greater impact of the mass media, the proximity of political life and struggles, the visibility of modern household appliances, laundries, etc.

5. In the colonial and semicolonial countries, women generally comprise a much lower percentage of the work force than in the imperialist countries. It tends to vary between 8 and 15 percent, although sometimes as high as 20 percent, as opposed to the advanced capitalist countries, where women make up roughly 30 to 40 percent.

As would be expected, women are concentrated in jobs that are the least skilled, lowest paying, and least protected by laws on safety conditions, minimum wages, etc. This is especially true for agricultural work, piecework in the home, and work as domestics, where a high proportion of women are employed. The average wage of female workers tends to be one-third to one-half of that of male workers. When women are able to get an education and acquire some skills, they are confined even more strictly than in the advanced capitalist countries to certain "female" occupations, such as nursing and teaching.

But women are also concentrated in industries such as textile, garment, food processing, and electrical parts and often make up a majority of the labor force employed there. Given the overwhelming predominance of such light industry in the more industrialized colonial countries, this means that, although they are a low percentage of the work force as a whole, women workers can occupy a strategically important place. In Puerto Rico, for example, women are the majority of the work force in the pharmaceutical and electrical industries, which are the major industries in the country.

The employment of women in such industries is crucial for the superprofits of the imperialists, both because they are a source of cheaper labor and also because the employment of women at lower wages or in lower-paying jobs allows the capitalists to divide and weaken the working class and keep down the overall wage scale. The process of imperialist accumulation cannot be fully understood without explaining the role of the superexploitation of women workers in the semicolonial countries.

Throughout the colonial world, unemployment and underemployment are of crisis proportions, and much of this burden falls on women. To help their family survive, women are often forced to resort to such desperate and precarious sources of income as selling handicrafts or home-cooked food in the streets, or taking in laundry. Prostitution is frequently the only recourse. The endemic unemployment also exacerbates alcoholism and drug addiction, which results in greater violence against women as well as even more desperate poverty.

6. In many colonial and semicolonial countries, women have not yet won some of the most elementary democratic rights secured by women in the advanced capitalist countries in the nineteenth and twentieth centuries. Numerous countries still retain laws that place women under the legal control of their male relatives. These include, for example, laws that require the husband's permission for a woman to work, laws that give the husband control over his wife's wages, and laws that give the husband automatic guardianship of his children and control over the residence of his wife. In some countries women are still sold into marriage. They can be murdered with impunity for violating the "honor" of their men.

In countries where reforms have been made in the legal code, providing women with more rights, these often remain largely formal. Women are unable to assert these rights in practice because of the crushing weight of poverty, illiteracy, malnutrition, their economic dependence, and backward traditions that circumscribe their lives. Thus imperialism in its death agony stands as an obstacle to the most elementary democratic rights for women in the colonial world.

7. The power and influence of organized religion is especially strong in the colonial and semicolonial countries, because of the prevailing economic backwardness and because of the reinforcement and protection of the religious hierarchies by imperialism. In many countries there is no separation of religious institutions and state. Even where there is official separation, religious dogma and customs retain great weight. For example, many of the most barbaric antiwomen laws are based on religious codes. In India, the misery of millions of women is accentuated by the caste system, which, though no longer sanctioned by law, is based on the Hindu religion. In Muslim countries, the tradition of the veiling of women, which is still quite prevalent, is designed to totally banish women from public life and deny them any individuality. In Catholic countries the right to divorce is often restricted or denied.

8. Violence against women, which has been inherent in their economic, social, and sexual degradation throughout all stages of development of class society, becomes accentuated by the contradictions bred under imperialist domination. The greater access of women to education and jobs, along with their broader participation in society in general, gives women the opportunities to lead a less protected, more public life, in violation of the old traditions and values. But attempts by women to take advantage of these opportunities and break out of the old roles often lead to reactions by male relatives or others, which can take the form of ostracism, beatings, mutilations, or even murder. Such barbaric violence against women is

frequently sanctioned by law. Even where illegal, it is often so widely accepted in practice that it goes unpunished.

9. Educational opportunities for women in the colonial and semicolonial countries remain extremely limited by comparison with the advanced capitalist countries. This is reflected in the high female illiteracy rate. From the level of primary school to the university level, female enrollment is lower than male, and the gap generally increases the higher the educational level.

The educational system in the colonial and semicolonial countries is organized—often more blatantly than in the imperialist countries—to reinforce the exclusion of women from social life and to bolster the imposition of the role of mother-housekeeper-wife on all female children. Coeducation is notably less prevalent, with the schools for girls invariably receiving smaller budgets, fewer teachers, and worse facilities. Where coeducation exists, girls are still required to pursue separate courses of study such as cooking, sewing, and homemaking.

Within the framework of these disadvantages, however, the pressure of the world market has brought some changes in the educational opportunities open to women. The need for a layer of more highly trained technicians has opened the doors to higher education for at least a small layer of women.

10. Women in the colonial world have even less control over their reproductive functions than women in the imperialist countries. The poor educational opportunities for females, combined with the strong influence of religion over the content of education, means that women have little or no access to scientific information about reproduction or sex. Economically and socially they are under personal pressure to produce more, not fewer children. When there is access to birth control information and devices, this is almost always in the framework of racist population control programs imposed by imperialism. In some countries forced sterilization of masses of women has been carried out by the government. In Puerto Rico the forced sterilization policies promoted by the U.S. government have victimized more than one-third of the women of child-bearing age. Forced sterilization schemes are foisted on oppressed groups within these countries as well, such as the Indian population of Bolivia.

Even in countries where forced sterilization is not official policy, the racist population control propaganda permeates society and constitutes an obstacle to the fight by women to gain control of their own bodies.

Women in semicolonial and colonial countries have been widely used as unwitting guinea pigs for testing birth control devices and drugs. And access to abortion, too, is tied to coercion, not freedom of choice. Each year, millions of women throughout the colonial world are forced to seek illegal abortions under the most unsanitary and degrading conditions possible, leading to an unknown number of deaths.

In all these ways, women are denied the right to choose when and if to bear children.

Under conditions of economic crisis, population control schemes will become more widespread and there will be more cases like Puerto Rico. The so-called "population explosion" will be blamed for the economic difficulties of the colonial and semicolonial countries in order to divert attention from the responsibility of imperialism for causing and maintaining this misery.

Racism and sexism are also imposed on the colonial world through the propagation of alien cultural standards. If the cosmetics merchants' standards of "beauty" for women in Europe and North America are oppressive to women in those areas, they are even more so when these same standards are foisted on women of the colonial and semicolonial countries through advertising, movies, and other forms of mass propaganda.

11. The strong influence of religion reinforces extreme backwardness regarding sexuality, which results in a special deprivation and degradation of women. The general proscription that women are supposed to be asexual themselves, but at the same time be a satisfying sexual slave to their husbands, is imposed more brutally on women in the colonial and semicolonial countries than in the imperialist countries, through traditions, laws, and the use of violence including the sexual mutilation of female children. Women are supposed to save their virginity for their husband. In many instances, if women do not provide sexual satisfaction to their husbands, or if they are charged with not being a

virgin at the time of marriage, this is grounds for divorce. The dual standard of sexual conduct for men and women is more strictly enforced than in the imperialist countries. The practice of polygamy is merely an extreme example.

Another reflection of the backwardness regarding sexuality is the harsh oppression of homosexuals, both male and female.

12. The fact that capitalist development in the colonial world incorporated precapitalist economic and social relations, many of which survive in distorted forms, means that to win their liberation, women, as well as all the oppressed and exploited, are confronted with combined tasks. The struggle against imperialist domination and capitalist exploitation often begins with the unresolved problems of national independence, land reform, and other democratic tasks.

Elementary democratic demands, such as those that give women rights as individuals independent of their husband's control, will have great weight in the struggle for women's liberation in the colonial and semicolonial countries. At the same time, they will immediately pose and be combined with social and economic issues whose solution requires the reorganization of all of society along socialist lines. Among such issues are rising prices, unemployment, inadequate health and educational facilities, and housing. They also include all the general demands that have been raised by the women's movement in the advanced capitalist countries, such as child-care centers, rights and medical facilities that would assure women the ability to control their reproductive lives, access to jobs and education. But none of these demands, including the most elementary democratic ones, can be won without the mobilization and organization of the working class, which constitutes the only social force capable of leading such struggles through to a victorious conclusion.

13. Because of the relative weakness of capitalism and of the ruling capitalist classes in the colonial and semicolonial countries, civil liberties, where they exist, are in general tenuous and often short-lived. Political repression is widespread. When women begin to struggle—as when other sectors of the population begin to rebel—they are often rapidly confronted with repression and with the necessity to fight for political liberties such as the right to hold meetings, to have their own organization, to have a newspaper or other publications, and to demonstrate. The struggle for women's liberation cannot be separated from the more general struggle for political freedoms.

The increased participation of women in social and political struggles has meant that women are a growing proportion of political prisoners in the colonial and semicolonial countries. In the prisons, women face particularly humiliating and brutal forms of torture. The struggle for freedom of all political prisoners, exposing the plight of women in particular, has been and will be an important part of the fight for women's liberation in these countries.

This struggle has an especially clear international dimension. Political prisoners exist not only in the colonial world but in the imperialist countries as well. Demands for their freedom will continue to be a rallying point for international solidarity within the women's movement.

14. The struggle for women's liberation has always been intertwined with the national liberation struggle. Whatever women do, they come up against the might of imperialist control, and the need to throw off the chains of this domination is an urgent and overriding task for all the oppressed in these countries, as the examples of Iran and Nicaragua have once again clearly demonstrated. Large numbers of women become politically active for the first time through participation in national liberation movements. In the process of the developing struggle, it becomes evident that women can and must play an even greater role if victory is to be won. Women become transformed by doing things that were forbidden to them by the old traditions and habits. They become fighters, leaders, organizers, and political thinkers. The deep contradictions they live with stimulate revolt against their oppression as a sex, as well as demands for greater equality within the revolutionary movement. In Vietnam, Algeria, Cuba, Palestine, South Africa, the Sahara, and elsewhere, struggles by women to end the most brutal forms of the oppression they suffer have been closely intertwined with unfolding anti-imperialist struggles.

In Nicaragua, women organized through AMPRONAC (Association of Women Confronting the National Problem) played a crucial role in preparing for the final insurrection against the Somoza dictatorship. And 30 percent of the FSLN's forces were composed of women who were organized in women's brigades as well as integrated in other combat and support units.

In Iran, the participation of women in the struggle to topple the Shah brought millions into social and political life for the first time, awakening in them the desire to change their own status as well. Despite the weight of reactionary religious ideas and antiwoman measures, the deepening of mass anti-imperialist consciousness and struggle in Iran can only improve the conditions under which women will fight for greater equality and freedom.

The participation of women in the national liberation struggle also begins to transform the consciousness of men about women's capacities and role. In the process of struggling against their own exploitation and oppression, men can become more sensitized to the oppression of women, more conscious of the necessity to combat it, and more aware of the importance of women as an allied fighting force.

15. There also exist oppressed national minorities *within* the colonial and semicolonial countries. In Iran, for example, the oppressed nationalities constitute 60 percent of the population. In Latin America, the native Indian population is an oppressed minority. The women of these minorities face a double dimension of national oppression. Once they begin to move, their struggle can develop in an explosive manner.

The demands of women and of oppressed nationalities will often be intertwined and reinforce one another. For example, the demand of all women for the right to an education will be combined with the demand of men and women of the oppressed nationalities for the right to education in their own languages.

16. Since the rise of the colonial revolution at the beginning of this century, women have participated in anti-imperialist upsurges, but there has not been a tradition of women organizing as women, around their specific demands, as a distinct component of these struggles. However, the development of the world capitalist system since World War II has sharpened the economic, social, and political contradictions in the colonial and semicolonial countries which will more and more propel women into struggle around their own demands.

a. In the period following World War II there was a rise in industrialization in the colonial and semicolonial countries, although the extent of this industrialization varied greatly in different countries and was distorted to fit the needs of the imperialist powers. This meant increased access by women to education and jobs.

b. Technological improvements in the areas of household tasks and control of reproduction—even though much less widely available than in the advanced countries—began to be known and showed the possibility of freeing women from domestic drudgery and allowing them to control their reproductive function.

c. The economic crisis of world capitalism which was signaled by the international depression of 1974–75 has had a magnified effect on the colonial world, as the imperialists attempted to foist the burden of this crisis onto the backs of the masses in these countries. A disproportionate weight of the economic crisis falls on women, in the form of rising prices, cutbacks in the rudimentary health and education facilities that exist, and increased misery in the countryside. Thus the gap between what is possible for women and what exists is widening.

d. The impact of this contradiction on the consciousness of women is reinforced today by the impact of the international women's liberation movement, which has inspired women around the world and popularized and legitimized their demands.

These factors point to the conclusion that struggles by women will become a more important component of the coming revolutionary struggles in the colonial and semicolonial countries.

This struggle by women can take on explosive dimensions due to the gap between the archaic norms and values and the possibilities for the liberation of women opened up by the technological advancements of capitalism. At the same time, the religious and traditional norms and values upheld by the imperialists and their servitors are in constant contradiction with the lives of growing numbers of women. This means that once women begin to challenge their oppression, even on an elementary level, it can combine with other social ferment and lead very rapidly to the mobilization of masses of women in struggles that take on a radical, anticapitalist direction.

17. Attitudes and policies concerning the demands and needs of women in colonial and semicolonial countries are one of the acid tests of the revolutionary caliber, perspective, and program of any organization aspiring to lead the struggle against imperialism. The role and importance that we ascribe to the fight for women's liberation in these countries, and the program we put forward for achieving it, separate us from nonproletarian forces contending for leadership of the national liberation struggle.

This has long been a distinguishing feature of the program of revolutionary Marxism, as was reflected in the resolutions of the Third and Fourth Congresses of the Communist International. These resolutions drew special attention to the exemplary work of the Chinese Communists in organizing and leading mobilizations of women that preceded the second Chinese revolution of 1925–27.

If the revolutionary Marxist party does not see the importance of organizing and mobilizing women and winning the leadership of the struggle for women's liberation, the field will be open for bourgeois and petty-bourgeois forces to succeed in gaining the leadership of women's movements and diverting them into reformist channels, or even into anti-working-class movements.

18. Only the road of the socialist revolution can open the way to a qualitative transformation in the lives of the masses of women of the semicolonial countries. The examples of Cuba, Vietnam, and China are a powerful beacon for the women of Asia, Africa, and Latin America. These socialist revolutions offer striking proof of the rapid advances possible once the working class in alliance with the peasantry breaks the chains of imperialist domination. When the laws of capitalist accumulation are replaced by those of a planned economy based on the nationalization of the decisive sectors of production, it becomes possible even in the impoverished countries of the semicolonial world to turn massive resources toward the development of education and childcare, medical services, and housing.

Once capitalism is eliminated, unemployment and underemployment become scourges of the past. On the contrary a shortage of labor draws women out of the home and into productive labor of all kinds in massive numbers. Social mores and traditions rooted in precapitalist and capitalist modes of production progressively disappear as this transformation develops and the working class becomes larger and more powerful.

19. Because of the extreme oppression they face, and the fact that there is no perspective for improving their lives under capitalism, women in the colonial and semicolonial countries will be thrust into the vanguard of the struggle for social change. Through internal classes and similar educational activities, sections of the Fourth International must systematically prepare their own members to understand the importance of the fight for women's liberation, even if there are no mass struggles on the political horizon as yet. We must take a conscious attitude toward winning women to socialism and training and integrating the most determined as leaders of our movement.

Women in the workers states: liberation betrayed

1. The October 1917 revolution in Russia and each subsequent socialist victory brought significant gains for women, including democratic rights and integration into the productive labor force. The measures enacted by the Bolsheviks under the leadership of Lenin and Trotsky demonstratively showed that the proletarian revolution meant immediate steps forward for women.

Between 1917 and 1927 the Soviet government passed a series of laws giving women legal equality with men for the first time. Marriage became a simple registration process that had to be based on mutual consent. The concept of illegitimacy was abolished. Free, legal abortion was made every woman's right. By 1927, marriages did not have to be registered, and divorce was granted on the request of either partner. Antihomosexual laws were eliminated.

Free, compulsory education to the age of 16 was established for all children of both sexes. Legislation gave women workers special maternity benefits.

The 1919 program of the Communist Party stated: "The party's task at the present moment is primarily work in the realm of ideas and education so as to destroy utterly all traces of the former inequality or prejudices, particularly among backward strata of the proletariat and peasantry. Not confining itself to formal equality of women, the party strives to liberate them from the material burdens of obsolete household work by replacing it by communal houses, public eating places, central laundries, nurseries, etc." This program was implemented to the extent possible given the economic backwardness and poverty of the new Soviet Republic, and the devastation caused by almost a decade of war and civil war.

A conscious attempt was made to begin combating the reactionary social norms and attitudes toward women, which reflected the reality of a country whose population was still overwhelmingly peasant, where women were a relatively small percentage of the work force, and in which the dead weight of feudal traditions and customs hung over all social relations. As would be expected under such conditions, backward attitudes toward women were reflected within the Bolshevik Party as well, not excepting its leadership. The party was by no means homogeneous in its understanding of the importance of carrying through the concrete and deepgoing measures necessary to fulfill its 1919 program.

2. The decimation and exhaustion of the working-class vanguard, and the crushing of the postwar revolutionary upsurges in Western Europe, laid the basis for the triumph of the counterrevolutionary bureaucratic caste, headed by Stalin, in the 1920s. While the economic foundations of the new workers state were not destroyed, a privileged social layer that appropriated for itself many of the benefits of the new economic order grew rapidly in the fertile soil of Russia's poverty. To protect and extend its new privileges, the bureaucracy reversed the policies of Lenin and Trotsky in virtually every sphere, from government based on soviet democracy, to control by the workers over economic planning, to the right of oppressed nationalities to self-determination, to a proletarian internationalist foreign policy.

By the late 1930s the counterrevolution had physically annihilated the entire surviving Bolshevik leadership and established a dictatorship that to this day keeps hundreds of thousands in prison camps, psychiatric hospitals, and exile, and ruthlessly crushes every murmur of opposition.

For women, the Stalinist counterrevolution led to a policy of reviving and fortifying the family system.

Trotsky described this process as follows: "Genuine emancipation of women is inconceivable without a general rise of economy and culture, without the destruction of the petty-bourgeois economic family unit, without the introduction of socialized food preparation and education. Meanwhile, guided by its conservative instinct, the bureaucracy has taken alarm at the 'disintegration' of the family. It began singing panegyrics to the family supper and the family laundry, that is, the household slavery of women. To cap it all, the bureaucracy has restored criminal punishments for abortions, officially returning women to the status of pack animals. In complete contradiction with the ABC of communism the ruling caste has thus restored the most reactionary and benighted nucleus of the class regime, i.e., the petty-bourgeois family" (*Writings of Leon Trotsky, 1937–38*, Pathfinder, 2nd ed., 1976, pp. 166-67 [2012 edition]).

3. The most important factor facilitating this retrogression was the cultural and material backwardness of Russian society, which did not have the resources necessary to construct adequate child-care centers, sufficient housing, public laundries, and housekeeping and dining facilities to eliminate the material basis for women's oppression. This backwardness also helped perpetuate the general social division of labor between men and women inherited from the tsarist period.

But beyond these objective limitations, the reactionary Stalinist bureaucracy consciously gave up the perspective of moving in a systematic way to socialize the burdens carried by women, and instead began to glorify the family system, attempting to bind families together through legal restrictions and economic compulsion.

As Trotsky pointed out in *The Revolution Betrayed*, "The retreat not only assumes forms of disgusting hypocrisy, but it also is going infinitely farther than the iron economic necessity demands."

The bureaucracy reinforced the family system for one of the same reasons it is maintained by capitalist society—as a means of inculcating attitudes of submission to authority and for perpetuating the privileges of a minority. Trotsky explained that "the most compelling motive of the present cult of the family is undoubtedly the need of the bureaucracy for a stable hierarchy of relations, and for the disciplining of youth by means of forty million points of support for authority and power."

As part of this counterrevolution, the old tsarist laws against homosexuality were dusted off and reintroduced.

Reinforcement of the family enabled the bureaucracy to perpetuate an important division inside the working class: the division between man, as "head of the family and breadwinner," and woman, as responsible for tasks inside the home and shopping—in addition to whatever else she might do. On a more general level, it meant maintaining the division between private life and public life, with the resulting isolation that affects both men and women. Bolstering of the nuclear family also reinforced the bureaucracy through encouraging the attitude of "each family for itself," and within the framework of a policy of overall planning that has little to do with satisfying the needs of the workers, it allows the bureaucracy to minimize the costs of social services.

The conditions created by the proletarian revolution and Stalinist counterrevolution in the Soviet Union have not been mechanically reproduced in all the deformed workers states of Eastern Europe and Asia. Important differences exist, reflecting historical, cultural, economic, and social variations from one country to another, even one region to another. However, despite differences of degree in the participation of women in the process of production or the extent of child-care centers and similar social services, maintenance of the economic and social inequality of women and policies aimed at reinforcing and justifying the domestic labor of women remain official policy in all the deformed workers states.

4. According to the official 1970 Soviet Union census, 90 percent of all urban women between the ages of 16 and 54 hold jobs outside the home. Yet the average Soviet woman spends four to seven hours a day on housework in addition to eight hours on an outside job.

The perpetuation of the responsibility of women for the domestic chores associated with child-raising, cooking, cleaning, laundry, and caring for the personal needs of other members of the family unit is the economic and social basis for the disadvantages and prejudices faced by women and the resulting discrimination in jobs and wages. This deeply affects the way women view themselves, their role in society, and the goals they seek to attain.

A survey made in Czechoslovakia at the end of the 1960s revealed that nearly 80 percent of women interviewed accepted the idea of staying in the home until their children reached the age of 3 years, if their husband agreed and if their income was sufficient to provide for the needs of the family. This is hardly surprising when one considers that, in the same period, out of 500 women interviewed who held supervisory positions on their jobs, half said they had to perform all of the domestic work in their homes (four or five hours per day).

While 50 percent of the wage earners in the Soviet Union are women, they are concentrated disproportionately in less-skilled, lower-paying, less responsible jobs, and in traditional female sectors of production and services. For example, 43.6 percent of all women still work in agriculture, while another quarter are employed in the textile industry. Eighty percent of all primary and secondary-school teachers, and 100 percent of all preschool teachers, are women. In 1970 only 6.6 percent of all industrial enterprises were headed by women. According to 1966 statistics, average women's wages in the Soviet Union were 69.3 percent of men's—up from 64.4 percent in 1924!

In 1970, in the East European countries as a whole, the salary differential ranged between 27 and 30 percent, despite the laws on equal pay that have been in effect for decades in these countries. This reflects the fact that women do not work the same jobs as men. Not only do they continue to be pushed toward the lower-paid "women's occupations," and not only are women often overqualified for the jobs they hold, but very few of those who complete apprenticeship programs for better-paying, more highly skilled jobs (notably, in heavy industry) continue working in these sectors. Domestic responsibilities make it difficult to keep up with new developments in one's specialty. Also protective laws establishing special conditions under which women can work often have discriminatory effects that prevent them from holding the same jobs as men.

In the Soviet Union in 1976, more than 40 percent of all scientists were women, but only 3 out of 243 full members of the Soviet Academy of Science were women. In the national political arena, only 8 of the 287 full members of the Communist Party Central Committee were women. There are no women in the Politburo.

In the Soviet Union and Eastern Europe, as in the advanced capitalist countries, sufficient material wealth and technology today exist to significantly alleviate the double burden of women. Yet the distortions introduced in economic planning and the productive process because of the absence of democratic control over production by the workers and the domination of the privileged bureaucratic caste are a source of resentments. Women feel the dead weight of the bureaucracy in this respect even more than men because they are forced to compensate for the distortions in the economy through the double day's labor they perform.

In the last decade, these potentially explosive resentments have forced the various bureaucratic castes to plan expanded production in consumer goods and increased social services. But the supply of consumer goods continues to lag behind the needs and growing expectations. Social services also remain sorely inadequate. For example, while child-care facilities are more widespread than in advanced capitalist countries, according to official figures in early 1978, child-care facilities in the Soviet Union could accommodate only 13 million of the more than 35 million preschool age children.

In Czechoslovakia and Poland at the beginning of the 1970s, only 10 percent of children under 3 could be accommodated in nurseries; of children between 3 and 6, there were places for only 37 and 45 percent, respectively. This is the case although women comprise between 40 and 45 percent of the work force in these two countries. Despite all the difficulties that such conditions create for working women, some of the Stalinist officials in these countries are reviving the theory of the "natural division of labor" between men and women. In Czechoslovakia and Hungary, the "solution" put forward to alleviate the lack of social services and at the same time attempt to reverse the declining birth rate is in essence a "salary for housework" allotted to mothers of one or two children until they reach the age of 3 years. This system is accompanied in Czechoslovakia by an increase in family allocations for the third and fourth child, as well as a substantial increase in the birth bonus for each child (which is nearly the equivalent of a month's salary). Obviously, such measures can only have the effect of pressing women to stay in the home, given the double day of work that accompanies having an outside job.

The number of public laundries is insignificant—in Czechoslovakia, Poland, and the USSR the existing laundries satisfy only 5–10 percent of the needs.

Similarly, the number of men and women workers who eat in public cafeterias has sharply decreased since the 1950s. Because of high prices and bad quality, only 20 percent of the population in Czechoslovakia eat their main meal outside the home—as opposed to 50 percent in earlier years.

All these conditions go in the direction of burying women in the home, a tendency fostered by the propaganda of the bureaucracy in favor of part-time work for women. This is expressed in East Germany, for example, in the extra day off each month given to women so they can do their housework. Of course, only women are given this "special privilege."

In October 1977 the same reactionary tendency was, in fact, incorporated into the revised Soviet constitution as an amendment to Article 35 that is supposed to guarantee equal rights to women. The amended constitution projects "the gradual shortening of the work-day for women with small children." Soviet leaders explained that this new constitutional provision reflected the line of the party and the Soviet state to improve the position of "women as workers, mothers, childraisers, and housewives."

This reinforcement of the social division of labor between men and women is also expressed through government policies in these countries aimed at increasing the birth rate to alleviate labor shortages. (East Germany is the only current exception.) At the same time that abortion has become more available to women in capitalist countries, the attempt to foster population growth has led to the restrictive measures concerning abortion throughout Eastern Europe.

In fact, the Stalinist bureaucracies have repudiated the view of Lenin and other leaders of the Russian revolution that unrestricted access to abortion is a woman's elementary democratic right. While legal abortion is generally available in the Soviet Union and Eastern Europe, the ruling castes have repeatedly curtailed this right, frequently placing humiliating conditions as well as economic penalties on women seeking abortions (such as denial of paid sick-leave time to obtain an abortion or refusal to cover abortions as a free medical procedure).

With the exception of Poland, sexual education and widespread information on contraceptive methods were explicitly rejected in most East European countries until very recently. Family planning centers were nonexistent, and access to contraceptive methods such as the pill or sterilization was strictly limited (in Czechoslovakia at the beginning of the 1970s, only 5 percent of women used such methods). But none of these measures have succeeded in reversing the continued stagnation in the birth rate or lowering the number of abortions. Faced with this "problem," the bureaucracy exercises great imagination in devising methods to encourage women to have more children. They consider everything *but* measures to socialize domestic tasks. In Poland, they are considering a "salary for housework," or a tax on the income of housewives who refuse to have children, or raising of the age of retirement for women from 60 to 65 years in order to release money for a maternity fund, or possibly lowering the retirement age for women to 55 years to enable them to help take care of small children.

In China, on the other hand, the Stalinist bureaucracy has introduced special economic penalties for couples with more than two children, in order to try to limit population growth. But the principle is the same. The right to choose is subordinated to the economic decisions made by the bureaucracy.

In all the Eastern European countries and in China the bureaucracy promotes policies aimed at reinforcing sexual repression. The extreme housing shortage, the kind of education given to children from earliest infancy, the frequent refusal to rent hotel rooms to non-married couples, pressure to postpone marriage, all reflect the dominant social mores and the bureaucracy's opposition to any form of sexual liberation. Given their place within the family, women are of course the first to feel the weight of these repressive norms and policies.

5. Women in the deformed and degenerated workers states will not win their full liberation short of a political revolution that removes the bureaucratic caste from power and restores workers democracy. Although there are as yet few signs of any rising consciousness concerning the oppression of women, there is no impenetrable barrier between the advanced capitalist countries and the workers states. Women in the workers states will inevitably be affected by the radicalization of women elsewhere and the demands they are raising.

The struggle of women for their liberation will be a significant component of the process of challenging and overturning the privileged bureaucratic regimes and establishing socialist democracy. Demands for the socialization of domestic labor in particular are an important aspect of the transitional program for the coming political revolution.

In some respects, in comparison with the capitalist countries, the economic independence and status of women in the workers states provide a positive contrast. But Soviet history also strikingly confirms the fact that the family institution is the cornerstone of the oppression of women. As long as women's domestic servitude is sustained and nurtured by economic and political policy, as long as the functions of the family are not fully taken over by superior social institutions, the truly equal integration of women in productive life and all social affairs is impossible. The responsibility of women for domestic labor is the source of the inequalities they face in daily life, in education, in work, and in politics.

6. The Stalinist counterrevolution in respect to women and the family, the vast inequality of women in the Soviet Union especially, more than 60 years after the October Revolution, today comprises one of the obstacles to winning radicalized women elsewhere to revolutionary Marxism. As with all other questions, the policies of Stalinism are often equated with Leninism rather than recognized for what they are—the negation of Leninism. Women fighting for their liberation elsewhere often look to the USSR and the deformed workers states and say, "If this is what socialism does for

Women factory workers in China.

women, we don't need it." Many anti-Marxists point to the situation of women in these countries as "proof" that the road to women's liberation is not through class struggle. Thus the fight to win the leadership of feminists in other parts of the world is interrelated with the development of the political revolution in the deformed and degenerated workers states, as well as with our ability to project a different image of the socialism we as authentic Marxists are fighting for.

II. THE FOURTH INTERNATIONAL AND THE STRUGGLE FOR WOMEN'S LIBERATION

Our perspective

1. The Fourth International welcomes and champions the emergence of a new wave of struggles by women to end their centuries-old oppression. By fighting in the front lines of these battles, we demonstrate that the world party of socialist revolution can provide a leadership capable of carrying the struggle for women's liberation through to its conclusion. Our goal is to win the confidence and leadership of the masses of women by showing that our program and our class-struggle policies will lead to the elimination of women's oppression along the path of successful proletarian revolution and the socialist reconstruction of society.

2. The perspective of the Fourth International stands in the long tradition of revolutionary Marxism. It is based on the following considerations:

a. The oppression of women emerged with the transition from preclass to class society. It is indispensable to the maintenance of class society in general and capitalism in particular. Therefore, struggle by masses of women against their oppression is a form of the struggle against capitalist rule.

b. Women are both a significant component of the working class, and a potentially powerful ally of the working class in the struggle to overthrow capitalism. Without the socialist revolution, women cannot establish the preconditions for their liberation. Without the mobilization of masses of women in struggle for their own liberation, the working class cannot accomplish its historic tasks.

The destruction of the bourgeois state, the eradication of capitalist property, the transformation of the economic bases and priorities of society, the consolidation of a new state power based on the democratic organization of the working class and its allies, and the continuing struggle to eliminate all forms of oppressive social relations inherited from class society—all this can ultimately be accomplished only with the conscious participation and leadership of an independent women's liberation movement.

Thus our support for building an independent women's liberation movement is part of the strategy of the revolutionary working-class party. It stems from the very character of women's oppression, the social divisions created by capitalism itself and the way these are used to divide and weaken the working class and its allies in the struggle to abolish class society.

c. All women are oppressed as women. Struggles around specific aspects of women's oppression necessarily involve women from different classes and social layers. Even some bourgeois women, revolting against their oppression as women, can break with their class and be won to the side of the revolutionary workers movement as the road to liberation.

As Lenin pointed out in his discussions with Clara Zetkin, action around aspects of women's oppression has the potential to reach into the heart of the enemy class, to "foment and increase unrest, uncertainty and contradictions and conflicts in the camp of the bourgeoisie and its reformist friends. . . . Every weakening of the enemy is tantamount to a strengthening of our forces."

Even more important from the point of view of the revolutionary Marxist party is the fact that resentment against their oppression as women can often be the starting point in the radicalization of decisive layers of petty-bourgeois women, whose support the working class must win.

d. While all women are oppressed, the effects of that oppression are different for women of different classes. Those who suffer the greatest economic exploitation are generally those who also suffer the most from their oppression as women. Thus the women's liberation movement provides an avenue to reach and mobilize many of the most oppressed and exploited women who might not otherwise be touched so rapidly by the struggles of the working class.

e. While all women are affected by their oppression as women, the mass women's liberation movement we strive to build must be basically working-class in composition, orientation, and leadership. Only such a movement, with roots in the most exploited layers of working-class women, will be able to carry the struggle for women's liberation through to the end in an uncompromising way, allying itself with the social forces whose class interests parallel and intersect those of women. Only such a movement will be able to play a progressive role under conditions of sharpening class polarization.

f. In this long-term perspective, struggles by women in the unions and on the job have a special importance, reflecting the vital interrelationship of the women's movement and the workers movement and their impact on each other.

This is testified to by the deepening radicalization of working-class women today, the growing understanding of forces in the women's liberation movement that they must orient to the struggles of working women, and the willingness of sections of the trade-union bureaucracy in some countries to begin to take a few initiatives around women's demands. All these developments point to the future character and composition of the women's liberation movement and the kind of class forces who will come forward to provide leadership.

g. Struggles by women against their oppression as a sex are interrelated with, but not totally dependent on or identical with, struggles by workers as a class. Women cannot win their liberation except in alliance with the organized power of the working class. But this historical necessity in no way means that women should postpone any of their struggles until the current labor officialdom is replaced by a revolutionary leadership that picks up the banner of women's liberation. Nor should women wait until the socialist revolution has created the material basis for ending their oppression. On the contrary, women fighting for their liberation must wait for no one to show them the way. They should take the lead in opening the fight and carrying it forward. In doing so they will play a leadership role within the workers movement as a whole, and can help create the kind of class-struggle leadership necessary to advance on all fronts.

h. Sexism is one of the most powerful weapons utilized by the ruling class to divide and weaken the workers movement. But it does not simply divide men against women. Its conservatizing weight cuts across sex lines, affecting both men and women.

Its hold is rooted in the class character of society itself, and the manifold ways in which bourgeois ideology is inculcated in every individual from birth. The bosses pit each section of the working class against all others. They promote the belief that women's equality can be achieved only at the *expense* of men—by taking men's jobs away from them, by lowering their wages, and by depriving them of domestic comforts. The reformist bureaucracy of the labor movement, of course, also plays upon these divisions to maintain its control.

Educating the masses of workers, male and female, through propaganda, agitation, and action around the needs of women is an essential part of the struggle to break the stranglehold of reactionary bourgeois ideology within the working class. It is an indispensable part of the politicalization and revolutionary education of the workers movement.

i. The full power and united strength of the working class can only be realized as the workers movement begins to overcome its deep internal divisions. This will only be achieved as the workers come to understand that those at the top of the wage scale do not owe their relative material advantages to the fact that others are discriminated against and specially oppressed. Rather it is the bosses who profit from such stratification and division. The class interests of *all* workers are identical with the demands and needs of the most oppressed and exploited layers of the class—the women, the oppressed nationalities, the immigrant workers, the youth, the unorganized, the unemployed. The women's movement has a particularly important role to play in helping the working class to understand this truth.

j. Winning the organized labor movement to fight for the demands of women is part of educating the working class to think socially and act politically. It is a central axis of the fight to transform the trade unions into instruments of revolutionary struggle in the interests of the entire working class.

In countering the efforts of the employers to keep the working class divided, we strive to win the ranks of the unions, and especially the young, combative rebels. The more successful we are in winning this battle, the more we will see the labor bureaucracy divide. Those who refuse to defend the interests of the great majority of the most oppressed and exploited will be progressively pushed aside.

The struggle by the revolutionary party to win hegemony and leadership in the working class is inseparable from the battle to convince the working class and its organizations to recognize and champion struggles by women as their own.

k. The struggle against the oppression of women is not a secondary or peripheral issue. It is a life-and-death matter for the workers movement, especially in a period of sharpening class polarization.

Because women's place in class society generates many deep-seated insecurities and fears, and because the ideology that buttresses women's inferior status still retains a powerful hold, especially outside the working class, women are a particular target for all clerical, reactionary, and fascist organizations. Whether it is the Christian Democrats, the Falange, or the opponents of abortion rights, reaction makes a special appeal to women for support, claiming to address women's particular needs, taking advantage of their economic dependence under capitalism, and promising to relieve the inordinate burden women bear during any period of social crisis.

From the "kinder-kirche-kueche" propaganda of the Nazi movement to the Christian Democrats' mobilization of middle-class women in Chile for the march of the empty pots in 1971, history has demonstrated time and again that the reactionary mystique of motherhood-and-family is one of the most powerful conservatizing weapons wielded by the ruling class.

Chile once again tragically showed that if the workers movement fails to put forward and fight for a program and revolutionary perspective answering the needs of the masses of women, many petty-bourgeois and even working-class women will either be mobilized on the side of reaction, or neutralized as potential supporters of the proletariat.

The objective changes in women's economic and social role, the new radicalization of women and the changes in consciousness and attitudes this has brought about, make it more difficult for reaction to prevail. This is a new source of revolutionary optimism for the working class. The mass explosion of feminist consciousness in Spain as one of the most significant components of the rising class struggle in the post-Franco era also demonstrates the speed with which the ideological hold of the church and state can begin to crumble in a period of revolutionary ferment, even in sectors of the population where it has been very strong.

l. While the victorious proletarian revolution can create the material foundations for the socialization of domestic labor and lay the basis for the complete economic and social equality of women, this socialist reconstruction of society, placing all human relations on a new foundation, will not be accomplished immediately or automatically. During the period of transition to socialism the fight to eradicate all forms of oppression inherited from class society will continue. For example, the social division of labor into feminine and masculine tasks must be eliminated in all spheres of activity from daily life to the factories. Decisions will have to be made concerning the allocation of scarce resources. An economic plan that reflects the social needs of women, and provides for the most rapid possible socialization of domestic tasks, will have to be developed. The continuing autonomous organization of women will be a precondition for democratically arriving at the correct economic and social decisions. Thus even after the revolution the independent women's liberation movement will play an indispensable role in assuring the ability of the working class as a whole, male and female, to carry this process through to a successful conclusion.

Our class-struggle strategy for the fight against women's oppression, our answer to the question of how to mobilize the working class on the side of women, and the masses of women on the side of the working class, has three facets: our political demands, our methods of struggle, and our class independence.

Our demands

Through the totality of the system of demands we put forward—which deal with every issue from freedom of political association, to unemployment and inflation, to abortion and child care, to workers control and the arming of the proletariat—we seek to build a bridge from the current needs and struggles of the working masses and their level of consciousness to the culminating point of socialist revolution. As part of this transitional program we put forward demands that speak to the specific oppression of women.

Our program points to the issues around which women can begin to struggle to loosen the bonds of their oppression and challenge the prerogatives of the ruling class. It recognizes and provides answers for all aspects of women's oppression—legal, economic, social, sexual.

We direct our demands against those responsible for the economic and social conditions in which women's oppression is rooted—the ruling class, its government and agencies. We orient the women's liberation movement toward clear political goals. We present our demands and propaganda in such a way as to show how a society no longer based on private property, exploitation, and oppression would radically transform the lives of women in all spheres.

Our interlocking set of tasks and slogans includes immediate, democratic, and transitional demands. Some can and will be wrested from the ruling class in the course of the struggle leading toward the socialist revolution. Such victories bring inspiration, increasing confidence, and self-reliance. Other demands will be partially met. The most fundamental will be resisted to the end by those who control the property and wealth. They can be won only in the course of the conquest of power and the socialist reconstruction of society.

In fighting for these demands—both those providing solutions to the specific oppression of women and those answering other needs of the oppressed nationalities and working class as a whole—masses of women will come to understand the interrelationship of their oppression as victims of class rule.

Our demands directed toward eliminating the specific oppression of women are centered on the following points:

1. *Full legal, political, and social equality for women.*

No discrimination on the basis of sex. For the right of all women to vote, engage in public activity, form or join political associations, live and travel where they want, engage in any occupations they choose. An end to all laws and regulations with special penalties for women. The extension to women of all democratic rights won by men.

2. *The right of women to control their own bodies.*

A woman has the sole right to choose whether or not to prevent or terminate pregnancy. This includes the rejection of population-control schemes which are tools of racism or class prejudice and which attempt to blame the evils of class society on the masses of working people and peasants.

a. An end to all government restrictions on abortion and contraception, including for minors, immigrant workers, and other noncitizens.

b. Free abortion on demand; no forced sterilization or any other government interference with the right of women to choose whether or when to bear children. Right to choose whatever method of abortion or contraception a woman prefers.

c. Free, widely disseminated birth control information and devices. State-financed birth control and sex education centers in schools, neighborhoods, hospitals, and factories.

d. Priority in medical research to development of totally safe, 100 percent effective contraceptives for men and women; an end to all medical and drug experimentation on women without their full, informed consent; nationalization of the drug industry.

3. *An end to the hypocrisy, debasement, and coercion of bourgeois and feudal family laws.*

a. Separation of church and state.

b. An end to all forced marriages and the buying and selling of wives. Abrogation of all laws against adultery. Abolition of laws giving men "conjugal rights" over their wives. An end to all laws, secular or religious, sanctioning penalties, physical abuse, or even murder of wives, sisters, and daughters for so-called crimes against male "honor."

c. Abolition of all laws forbidding marriage between men and women of different races, religions, or nationalities.

d. Marriage to be a voluntary process of civil registration.

e. The right to automatic divorce on request of either partner. State provision for economic welfare and job training for the divorced woman.

f. Abolition of the concept of "illegitimacy." An end to all discrimination against unwed mothers and their children. An end to the prisonlike conditions that govern special centers set up to take care of unwed mothers and other women who have nowhere else to go.

g. The rearing, social welfare, and education of children to be the responsibility of society, rather than the burden of individual parents. Abolition of all laws granting parents property rights and total control over children. Strict laws against child abuse.

h. An end to all laws victimizing prostitutes. An end to all laws reinforcing the double standard for men and women in sexual matters. An end to all laws and regulations victimizing youth for sexual activities.

i. An end to the mutilation of women through the practice of infibulation or clitorectomy.

j. Abrogation of all antihomosexual laws. An end to all discrimination against homosexuals in employment, housing, child custody. An end to the insulting stereotyping of homosexuals in textbooks and mass media, or portrayal of homosexual relations as perverted and against nature.

k. Violence against women—often sanctioned by reactionary family laws—is a daily reality that all women experience in some form. If it is not the extreme of rape or beatings, there is still the ever present threat of sexual assault implicit in the widespread circulation of pornographic literature, and the obscene comments and gestures women are constantly subjected to in the streets and on the job.

We demand the elimination of laws predicated on the assumption that female rape victims are the guilty party; establishment of centers—independent of the police and courts—designed to welcome, counsel, and help battered wives, rape victims, and other female victims of sexual violence; improvement of public transportation, street lighting, and other public services that make it safer for women to go out alone.

Violence against women is a vicious product of the general social and economic conditions of class society. It inevitably increases during periods of social crisis. But we strive to educate women and men that sexual violence cannot be eradicated without changing the foundation from which the economic, social, and sexual degradation of women flows. We expose the racist and anti–working class use of antirape laws to victimize men of oppressed nationalities. We oppose demands raised by some feminists to inflict drastic penalties on convicted rapists or to strengthen the repressive apparatus of the state, whose cops are among the most notorious brutalizers of women.

We oppose any kind of censorship of literature, even under the guise of campaigns against pornography.

4. *Full economic independence for women.*

a. Guaranteed jobs at union wages for all women who want to work, coupled with a sliding scale of hours and wages to combat inflation and unemployment among men and women. A shorter workweek for all.

b. Elimination of laws that discriminate against women's right to receive and dispose of their own wages and property.

c. Equal pay for equal work. For a national minimum wage based on union scale.

d. No discrimination against women in any trade, profession, job category, apprenticeship, or training program.

e. Preferential hiring, training, job upgrading, and seniority adjustments for women and other superexploited layers of the labor force in order to overcome the effects of decades of systematic discrimination against them. No preferential hiring for men in traditionally female-dominated trades and industries.

f. Paid maternity leaves for father and mother with no loss of job or seniority.

g. Paid work leaves to care for sick children to be given to men and women alike.

h. The extension of beneficial protective legislation (providing special working conditions to women) to cover men, in order to improve working conditions for both men and women and prevent the use of protective legislation to discriminate against women.

i. A uniform retirement age for men and women, with each individual free to take retirement or not.

j. Part-time workers to be guaranteed the same hourly wages and benefits as full-time workers.

k. Compensation at union rates throughout periods of unemployment for all women and men, including youth who cannot find a place in the work force, regardless of marital status, or previous employment record. Unemployment compensation to be protected against inflation by automatic increases.

5. *Equal educational opportunities.*

a. Free, open admissions for all women to all institutions of education and all programs of study, including on-the-job training programs. Special preferential admissions programs to encourage women to enter traditionally male-dominated fields and learn skills and trades from which they have previously been excluded.

b. An end to all forms of pressuring women to prepare themselves for "women's work," such as homemaking, secretarial work, nursing, and teaching.

c. Special education and refresher courses to aid women reentering the job market.

d. An end to portrayal in textbooks and mass media of women as sex objects and stupid, weak, emotionally dependent creatures. Courses designed to teach the true history of women's struggles against their oppression. Physical education courses to teach women to develop their strength and be proud of their athletic abilities.

e. No expulsion of pregnant students or unwed mothers, or segregation into special facilities.

6. *Reorganization of society to eliminate domestic slavery of women.*

The family as an economic unit cannot be "abolished" by fiat. It can only be replaced over time. The goal of the socialist revolution is to create economic and social alternatives that are superior to the present family institution and better able to provide for the needs currently met, however poorly, by the family, so that personal relationships will be a matter of free choice and not of economic compulsion. To ultraleft propaganda and agitation for the "abolition" of the family, we counterpose:

a. Free, government-financed twenty-four-hour childcare centers and schools, conveniently located and open to all children from infancy to early adolescence regardless of parents' income, employment situation, or marital status; trained male and female personnel; elimination of all sexist educational practices; child-care policies to be decided by those who use the centers.

b. Free medical care for all and special child-care facilities for children who are ill.

c. Systematic development of low-cost, high-quality social services such as cafeterias, restaurants, and take-out food centers available to all;

collective laundry facilities; housecleaning services organized on an industrial basis.

d. A crash, government-financed development program to provide healthful, uncrowded housing for all; no rent to exceed 10 percent of income; no discrimination against single women or women with children.

These demands indicate the issues around which women will fight for their liberation, and show how this fight is interrelated with the demands raised by other oppressed sectors of society and the needs of the working class as a whole. It is in struggle along these lines that the working class will be educated to understand and oppose sexism in all its forms and expressions.

The women's liberation movement raises many issues. The development of the movement has already demonstrated that not all will come to the fore with equal force at any given time. Which demands to raise at any particular time in the course of a particular struggle, the best way to formulate specific demands so that they are understandable to the masses and able to mobilize them in action, when to advance new demands to move the struggle forward—the answer to those tactical problems is the function of the revolutionary party, the art of politics itself.

Our methods of struggle

1. We utilize proletarian methods of mobilization and action in order to achieve these demands. Everything we do is geared to bring the masses themselves into motion, into struggle, whatever their current level of consciousness. The masses do not learn simply by being exposed to ideas or by the exemplary action of others. Only through their own direct involvement will the political consciousness of the masses develop, grow, and be transformed. Only through their own experience will millions of women be won as allies in the revolutionary struggle and come to understand the need to get rid of an economic system based on exploitation.

Our goal is to teach the masses to rely on their own united power. We utilize elections and other institutions of bourgeois democracy to clearly present our program to the broadest possible numbers of workers. But we counterpose extraparliamentary mass action—demonstrations, meetings, strikes, occupations—to reliance on elections, lobbying, parliaments, legislatures, and the bourgeois and petty-bourgeois politicians who haunt them.

Our class-struggle methods are geared to awakening the initiatives of the great majority of women; to bring them together; to destroy their domestic isolation and their lack of confidence in their own abilities, intelligence, independence, and strength. Struggling together with them, we aim to show that class exploitation is the root of women's oppression and its elimination the only road to emancipation.

Just as we strive to develop the class consciousness of the women's liberation movement, we try to win the workers movement to take up the struggle against each aspect of women's oppression.

In every struggle, we aim to educate women to understand the class inequality that sharpens the oppression of the most exploited. We try to lead the movement to address itself first and foremost to mobilizing women of the working class and oppressed nationalities. Through the system of demands we advance and the propaganda we put forward, we strive to move the struggle in an anticapitalist direction. We highlight the social implications of demands and expose the logic of profit and the conditions of class society that limit the capacity of the ruling class to implement in practice even the concessions wrung from it through struggle.

2. The oppression of women as a sex constitutes the objective basis for the mobilization of women in struggle through their own organizations. For that reason the Fourth International supports and helps build the women's liberation movement.

By the women's movement we mean all the women who organize themselves at one level or another to struggle against the oppression imposed on them by this society: women's liberation groups, consciousness-raising groups, neighborhood groups, student groups, groups organized at workplaces, trade-union commissions, organizations of women of oppressed nationalities, lesbian-feminist groups, action coalitions around specific demands. The women's movement is characterized by its heterogeneity, its penetration into all layers of society, and the fact that it is not tied to any particular political organization, even though various currents are active within it. Moreover, some groups and action coalitions, though led and sustained by women, are open to men as well, such as the National Organization for Women in the United States and the National Abortion Campaign in Britain.

While most women's groups initially developed outside the mass organizations of the working class, the deepening radicalization has led more and more working-class women to find ways to organize themselves within their class organizations. In Spain, large numbers of women joined the COs (Workers' Commissions) and brought life to their women's committees. In France, thousands of women now participate in trade-union commissions as well as Family Planning organizations and women's groups. In Bolivia, miners' wives have formed housewives' committees affiliated to the COB (Bolivian Workers Federation).

But all these are forms of the turbulent and still largely unstructured reality called the independent or autonomous women's movement.

By independent or autonomous we do not mean independent of the class struggle or the needs of the working class. On the contrary, only by fusing the objectives and demands of the women's movement with the struggle of the working class will the necessary forces be assembled to achieve women's goals.

By independent or autonomous we mean that the movement is organized and led by women; that it takes the fight for women's rights and needs as its first priority, refusing to subordinate that fight to any other interests; that it is not subordinate to the decisions or policy needs of any political tendency or any other social group; that it is willing to carry through the fight by whatever means and together with whatever forces prove necessary.

Clearly, not every group within the movement measures up to those criteria fully or equally, but such is the character of the independent women's liberation movement we seek to build.

3. The dominant organizational form of the women's movement has been all-female groups. These have emerged in virtually all arenas from the schools and churches to the factories and trade unions. This expresses the determination of women to take the leadership of their own organizations in which they can learn and develop and lead without fear of being put down or dictated to by men or having to compete with them from the start.

Before women can lead others they must throw off their feelings of inferiority and self-deprecation. They must learn to lead themselves. Feminist groups that consciously and deliberately exclude men help many women to take the first steps toward discarding their own slave mentality, gaining confidence, pride, and courage to act as political beings.

The small "consciousness raising" groups that have emerged everywhere as one of the most prevalent forms of the new radicalization help many women to realize that their problems do not arise from personal shortcomings, but are socially created and common to other women.

If they remain inward-turned and limit themselves to discussion circles as a substitute for joining with others to act, they can become an obstacle to the further political development of the women involved. But they most often lay the groundwork for women to break out of their isolation for the first time, to gain confidence, and to move into action.

The desire of women to organize themselves in all-female groups is the opposite of the practice followed by many mass Stalinist parties that organize separate male and female youth organizations for the purpose of repressing sexual activity and reinforcing sex-stereotyped behavior—i.e., the inferiority of women. The independent all-female groups that have emerged today express in part the distrust many radicalizing women feel for the mass reformist organizations of the working class, which have failed so miserably to fight for their needs.

Our support for and work to build the independent women's liberation movement distinguishes the Fourth International today from many sectarian groups that claim to stand on Marxist orthodoxy as represented by their interpretations of the resolutions of the first four congresses of the Third International. Such groups reject the construction of any women's organizations except those tied directly to and under the political control of their party.

To those "Marxists" who claim that women's liberation groups organized on the basis of women only divide the working class along sex lines, we say it is not those fighting against their oppression who are responsible for creating or maintaining divisions. Capitalism divides the working class—by race, by sex, by age, by nationality, by skill levels, and by every other means possible. Our job is to organize and support the battles of the most oppressed and exploited layers who are raising demands that represent the interests of the entire class and who will lead the struggle for socialism. Those who suffer most from the old will fight the most energetically for the new.

4. The forms through which we work can vary greatly depending on the concrete circumstances in which our organizations find themselves. Our tactics are dictated by our strategic aim, which is to educate and lead in action forces much broader than ourselves, especially the decisive forces of the working class, to help build a mass women's liberation movement, to strengthen a class-struggle wing of the women's movement, and to recruit the best cadre to the revolutionary party.

Factors that must be taken into account include the strength of our own forces; the size, character, and political level of the women's liberation forces; the strength of the liberal, Social Democratic, Stalinist, and centrist forces against whom we must contend; and the general political context in which we are working. It's a tactical question whether we should organize women's liberation groups on a broad socialist program, work through existing organizations of the women's liberation movement, build broad action coalitions around specific issues, work through trade-union commissions or caucuses in other mass organizations, combine several of these activities, or work through some altogether different forms.

No matter what organizational form we adopt, the fundamental question to be decided is the same: What specific issues and demands should be raised under the given circumstances in order to most effectively mobilize women and their allies in struggle?

5. There is no contradiction between supporting and building all-female organizations to fight for women's liberation, or for specific demands relating to women's oppression, and simultaneously building mass action coalitions involving both men and women to fight for the same demands. Campaigns around the right to abortion have provided a good example of this. Women will be the backbone of such campaigns, but since the fight is in the interests of the working masses as a whole, our perspective is to win support for the movement from all organizations of the working class and the oppressed.

6. Our perspective of trying to mobilize masses of women in action can often best be achieved in the present period through united-front-type action campaigns, which mobilize the broadest possible support around concrete demands. This is all the more true, given the relative weakness of the sections of the Fourth International and the relative strength of the liberals and our reformist, class-collaborationist opponents. For many women and men, participation in the actions organized by such campaigns has been their first step toward support for the political goals of the women's liberation movement. The united-front-type abortion campaigns in numerous countries provide an example of this type of action.

Through such united-front-type actions we can bring the greatest power to bear against the capitalist government and educate women and the working class concerning their own strength. Insofar as the liberal "friends" of women, the Stalinists, Social Democrats, and trade-union bureaucrats refuse to support such united campaigns for women's needs, they will isolate and expose themselves by their own inaction, opposition, or willingness to subordinate women's needs to their search for an alliance with the supposedly "progressive" sectors of the ruling class. And if mass pressure obliges them to support such actions, this can only broaden the mass appeal of the campaigns and increase the contradictions within the reformist and liberal forces.

As we have already seen so clearly around the abortion question, such united-front-type action campaigns are of particular importance in deepening the interaction between the independent women's movement and the labor movement, since they put the greatest pressure on the labor bureaucracy to respond.

7. Because our orientation is to build a women's movement that is basically working-class in composition and leadership, and because of the interconnection between the fight for women's

liberation and the transformation of the trade unions into instruments that effectively defend the interests of the whole class, we give special importance to struggles by women in the unions and on the job. Our aim is to organize women to actively participate in their unions and in the women's liberation movement.

Here as elsewhere in capitalist society, women are subject to male domination, to discrimination as an inferior sex that is out of its "natural place." But the growing number of women in the work force and their deepening consciousness of their double oppression, have already brought significant changes in the attitudes of working women, strengthening their inclination to organize, unionize, and fight for their rights.

Women workers are involved in many struggles for general demands relating to the economic needs and job conditions of all workers. They also frequently raise the special needs of women workers such as equal pay, maternity benefits, child-care facilities, and preferential hiring and training. Both are central to the struggle for women's liberation as well as to the working class in general. Such struggles and demands by women workers will assume a greater weight as the class struggle deepens under the impact of the economic crisis. They will have a greater and greater impact on the women's liberation movement.

Most women who enter into such struggles do not think of themselves as feminists. They simply think they are entitled to equal pay for doing the same job as a man, or believe they have a right to be employed in some traditionally "masculine" line of work. They often protest vigorously that they are not feminists.

Working women who become involved in struggles on the job confront the same issues and conditions that have given rise to the independent women's movement.

They often face sexist harassment and abuse which is organized and promoted by their foremen and supervisors. Even when it comes from their fellow workers, it is often the result of an atmosphere fostered by the employer. Women face the sometimes difficult job of fighting to convince the union to defend them against serious harassment and victimization by management personnel. They have to convince fellow workers that when they give women a hard time on the job, they are only doing the boss's job for him, and playing into his divide-and-rule tactics.

As women begin to play an active role, to take on leadership responsibilities, to prove their leadership capacities to themselves and others, to gain confidence and play an independent role, they develop a greater understanding of what the women's liberation movement is fighting for. The correct presentation of clear, concrete demands and objectives by the feminist movement is indispensable in reaching and involving millions of working women whose conscious political development begins as they try to confront their problems as women who must also work a job to earn a living.

8. The growing weight and role of women in the labor movement has an important impact on the consciousness of many male workers, who begin to see women more as equal partners in struggle and less as weak creatures who must be coddled and protected.

In this context, demands for preferential hiring, training, and job promotion for women in the traditionally male-dominated sectors of the economy have a special importance.

a. They challenge the division within the working class along sex lines, divisions that are fostered and maintained by the bosses in order to weaken the working class and hold down the wages and working conditions of the entire class.

b. They help educate both male and female workers to appreciate the material effects of discrimination against women, and the need for conscious measures to overcome the effects of centuries of enforced subjugation.

c. As women begin to break down the traditional division of labor along sex lines and establish their equal right to employment and their ability to perform "male" jobs as well as men, sexist attitudes and assumptions within the working class are undercut and the social division of labor in all spheres is challenged.

Struggles that open the doors for women to enter the educational, occupational, and leadership realms previously dominated by men pose in the clearest possible manner the eradication of women's inferior social status. Along with demands that raise the basic democratic rights of women, and those that go toward socializing the domestic labor women perform, such as the expansion and improvement of child-care facilities, they have a powerful educational impact within the working class.

9. Such demands also have a special importance as part of the fight to transform the unions into revolutionary instruments of class struggle and challenge the sexist bias of the labor bureaucracy. The union bureaucracy bases itself on the most privileged layers of male workers, who usually see preferential demands as a threat to their immediate prerogatives. The most conscious elements of the bureaucracy thus adamantly oppose those demands raised by the most oppressed and exploited sectors of the working class which are aimed at eradicating the deep divisions within the class.

An important part of our strategic orientation to develop a class-struggle left wing in the trade-union movement is to utilize the growing weight of forces like the women's liberation movement to pose the key social and political issues on which the labor movement should be playing a leadership role.

As the ranks of the unions are won to support such struggles the reactionary antiwoman and therefore anti–working class policies of the labor bureaucracy will be exposed and new forces will come forward to lead.

10. There are many difficulties in organizing women workers. Precisely because of their oppression as women, they are less likely to be unionized or to have a strong class consciousness. Their participation in the labor force is frequently more sporadic. Their double burden of responsibilities and chores at home is fatiguing and time-consuming, leaving them less energy for political and trade-union activity. The gross inadequacy of child-care facilities makes participation in meetings especially difficult.

For these reasons, the fight to convince the trade unions to take up the special demands of women is inseparable from the fight for trade-union democracy. Trade-union democracy includes not only issues such as the right of the membership to vote on all questions, election of all leadership bodies and personnel, and the right to form tendencies. It also implies special measures that permit women to participate with full equality—child-care facilities organized by the union during meetings, union commissions that deal specifically with women's needs, the right to meet in women's caucuses when necessary, special provisions to meet during working hours, and measures to assure adequate representation of women on all leadership bodies. Within the workers movement, challenging sexist attitudes and practices is an integral part of the fight for trade-union democracy and class solidarity.

11. If we give special importance to the struggles of women working outside the home it is not because we deprecate the oppression suffered by housewives. On the contrary, we understand and put forward a program that answers the deep problems faced by women in the home, the overwhelming majority of whom are working-class women, who will spend some part of their life in the labor market in addition to carrying out their domestic responsibilities. We offer a perspective of escape from the mind-deadening drudgery of housework, the isolation it imposes on each individual woman, the economic dependence of housewives, and the fear and insecurity this produces. We counterpose our program of socialization of housework and the integration of women into the productive labor force on an equal basis to the alternatives offered by reaction—a glorification of housework and motherhood and proposals to compensate women for their domestic slavery through wages for housework or similar superficially alluring schemes.

As capitalism in crisis shifts more and more economic burdens onto the individual family, it is often housewives, responsible for trying to stretch the family income to cover the basic necessities, who first take to the streets in protest over food shortages and soaring inflation. Such movements can be a first step toward political consciousness and collective action for thousands of women. They offer an opening and a challenge to the labor movement to join with and help provide leadership and direction for such protests—which can develop with explosive rapidity. Demands for joint worker-consumer price surveillance committees provide common ground for the labor movement, protesting housewives, and other consumers.

Unlike housewives, however, working women are already semiorganized by the labor market.

Their place within the working class, within the workers movement, and their economic status put them in a position to play a pivotal leadership role in the struggles of women and of the working class as a whole.

12. There is no contradiction between building the independent women's liberation movement, building trade unions, and building a revolutionary Marxist party of women and men.

The struggle for socialism requires all three. They serve different functions. The mass feminist movement mobilizes women in struggle around their needs and through their own independent forms of organization. The trade unions are the basic economic defense organizations of the working class. The mass revolutionary Marxist party, through program and action, provides leadership for the working class and its allies, including women, and uncompromisingly orients all facets of the class struggle toward a combined drive to establish a workers government and abolish capitalism.

There is no objective basis for a separate revolutionary Marxist women's organization. Unless women and men share equally in the rights and responsibilities of membership and leadership in a party that develops a political program and activities that represent the interests of all the oppressed and exploited, the party can never lead the working class to accomplish its historic tasks.

We maintain that there are no exclusively "women's issues." Every question of concern to the female half of humanity is likewise a broader social question of vital interest to the working class as a whole. While we raise demands that deal with the specific oppression of women, we have no separate program for women's liberation. Our demands are an integral part of our transitional program for the socialist revolution.

13. The program of the revolutionary party synthesizes the lessons of struggles against all forms of economic and social exploitation and oppression. The party expresses the historic interests of the proletariat through its program and action. Thus it not only learns from the participation of its members in the women's liberation movement. It also has an indispensable role to play. Through our work to build the independent women's movement, we deepen the party's understanding of women's oppression and the struggle against it. And we also strive to win ever greater forces to an effective strategy for women's liberation, that is, to a class-struggle perspective.

We do not demand agreement with our program as a precondition for building the independent women's movement. On the contrary, a broad-based movement, within which a wide range of personal experiences and political perspectives can contend in a framework of democratic debate and discussion, can only strengthen the political confidence and combativity of the movement. It enhances the possibility of developing a correct perspective.

However, we do not strive for the organic unity of all components of the women's movement at all costs. We fight for the broadest possible unity *in action* on the basis of demands and activities that genuinely reflect the objective needs of women, which is also the program in the interests of the working class.

We try to build the strongest possible wing within the women's liberation movement of those who share our class-struggle perspectives. A consistent struggle against all aspects of women's oppression means resolutely combatting all attempts to divert women's struggles into the reformist dead end of managing the rulers' austerity programs, or towards a search for individual solutions. We strive to recruit the most conscious and combative to the revolutionary party.

Our goal is to win the leadership of the women's liberation movement by showing women in practice that we have the program and perspectives that can lead to liberation. This is not a sectarian stance. Nor does it indicate a manipulative attempt to dominate or control the mass movement. On the contrary, it reflects our conviction that the struggle against women's oppression can be won only if the feminist movement develops in an anticapitalist direction. Such an evolution is not automatic. It depends on the demands put forward, the class forces toward which the feminist movement orients, and the forms of action in which it engages. Only the conscious intervention of the revolutionary party and its ability to win the confidence and leadership of women fighting for their liberation offers any guarantee that the women's struggle will ultimately be victorious.

14. We are concerned with all aspects of women's oppression. However, as a political party based on a program that represents the historic interests of the working class and all the oppressed, our prime task is to help direct the women's liberation movement toward political action that can effectively lead to the eradication of private property in which that oppression is rooted. Around every facet of women's oppression we strive to develop demands and actions that challenge the social and economic policies of the bourgeoisie and point toward the solutions that would be possible were it not for the fact that all social policies are decided on the basis of maximizing private profits.

Our approach to the struggle for women's liberation as an eminently political question often brings us into conflict with petty-bourgeois radical-feminist currents, who counterpose the development of new individual "life-styles" to political action directed against the state. They blame men instead of capitalism. They counterpose reforming men as individuals, trying to make them less sexist, to organizing against the bourgeois government which defends and sustains the institutions of class society responsible for male supremacy and women's oppression. They often attempt to build utopian "counterinstitutions" in the midst of class society.

As revolutionists we recognize that the problems many women seek to resolve in this way are real and preoccupying. Our criticism is not directed against individuals who try to find a personal way out from under the intolerable pressures capitalist society places on them. But we point out that for the masses of workers there is no "individual" solution. They must fight collectively to change society before their "life-style" will be significantly altered. Ultimately there are no purely private solutions for any of us. Individual escapism is a form of utopianism that can only end in disillusionment and the dispersal of revolutionary forces.

Our class independence

1. Political independence is the third facet of our class-struggle strategy for the fight against women's oppression. We do not defer or subordinate any demand, action, or struggle of women to the political needs and concerns of either the bourgeois or reformist political forces with their parliamentary shadowboxing and electoral maneuvers.

2. We fight to keep women's liberation organizations and struggles independent of all bourgeois forces and parties. We oppose attempts to divert women's struggles toward the construction of women's caucuses inside of or oriented to capitalist parties or bourgeois politics, as has occurred in the United States, Canada, and Australia. We oppose the formation of a women's political party, such as arose in Belgium and has been advocated by some feminist groups in Spain and elsewhere. The election of more women to public office on a liberal-bourgeois or radical petty-bourgeois program, while a reflection of changing attitudes, can do nothing to further the interests of women.

Women's liberation is part of the historic struggle of the working class against capitalism. We strive to make that link a conscious one on the part of women and of the working class. But we do not reject support from bourgeois figures or politicians who voice their agreement with any of our demands or goals. That strengthens our side, not theirs. It is their contradiction, not ours.

3. We strive for united-front action on specific demands and campaigns with the broadest possible forces, especially the mass reformist parties of the working class. But we reject the political perspectives of the Stalinist and Social Democratic parties.

The policies and conduct of both these currents within the working-class movement are based on preserving the institutions of the capitalist system, including the family, regardless of any lip service they may pay to the struggles of women against their oppression. Both are ready to subordinate the needs of women to whatever class-collaborationist deal they are trying to negotiate at the moment, whether it be with the monarchy in Spain, the Christian Democrats in Italy, or the bourgeois opposition parties in West Germany or Britain. The Stalinists never tire of telling women that the road to happiness is through "advanced democracy" or the "antimonopoly coalition." They advise women not to demand more than "democracy" (i.e., capitalism) can give. The Social Democrats, especially when they are managing "austerity" programs for the bourgeoisie, are never slow to implement the cutbacks in social services demanded by the ruling class, measures that frequently hit women the hardest.

4. It is only through an uncompromising programmatic and organizational break from the bourgeoisie and all forms of class collaborationism that the working class and its allies, including women struggling for their liberation, can be mobilized as a powerful and self-confident force capable of carrying the socialist revolution through to the end. The task of the revolutionary Marxist party is to provide the leadership to educate the working masses, including the women's movement, through action and propaganda in this class-struggle perspective.

Tasks of the Fourth International today

1. The new rise of the women's liberation movement has proceeded unevenly on a world scale, and feminist consciousness has had varying degrees of impact. But the speed with which revolutionary ideas and lessons of struggle are transmitted from one country to another, and from one sector of the world revolution to another, ensures the continuing spread of women's liberation struggles. Increasingly widespread questioning of the traditional role of women creates an atmosphere conducive to Marxist education and propaganda, as well as concrete action in support of the liberation of women. Through our press and propaganda activities the Fourth International has growing opportunities to explain the source and nature of women's oppression, our program for eradicating that oppression along with the class society in which it is rooted, and the revolutionary dynamic of women's struggle for liberation.

2. The involvement of our sections and sympathizing organizations in the women's liberation movement in numerous countries has shown that considerable potential exists for helping to organize and lead action campaigns around issues raised in the struggle against women's oppression. Such campaigns often provide opportunities especially for our women comrades to gain valuable experience and to play a leadership role in the mass movement. They are frequently an avenue through which even relatively small numbers of comrades can play a significant political role and win influence among much broader forces. Our support for and active participation in the women's liberation movement has already won us many new members.

The orientation of the sections and sympathizing organizations of the Fourth International is to commit our forces to building the women's liberation movement and action campaigns around specific issues like abortion, child care, the right to a job, and other aspects of our program.

We also encourage international solidarity in the women's movement, and where possible, international coordination of action campaigns around common issues. The international campaign on abortion rights, in which our sections have frequently played a decisive role, is a good example of the type of international coordination that is possible.

3. In addition to participating in all the various independent organizational forms that have emerged as part of the radicalization of women, we must integrate women's liberation propaganda and activity into all our areas of work, from the trade unions to the student milieu. It is especially among the youth—students, young workers, young housewives—that we will find the greatest receptivity to our ideas and program and readiness for action.

Women's liberation work is not the responsibility of women comrades alone, although they will have to lead it. As with every other question, the entire membership and leadership of the party must be knowledgeable about our work, collectively participate in determining our political line, and take responsibility for carrying our campaigns and propaganda into all areas of the class struggle where we are active. Male as well as female comrades will help to drive this forward.

4. To organize and carry out systematic women's liberation work, sections of the Fourth International should establish commissions or fractions composed of those involved in this work. Such fractions would include male as well as female comrades depending on the activities in which we are involved.

They should help the appropriate leadership bodies to give regular attention to all aspects of our work around issues and demands raised by the women's liberation movement, including proposals for internal education of our own membership. By establishing such commissions and fractions which—together with the leadership bodies—are responsible for discussing and implementing systematic work we can take maximum advantage of the opportunities and openings, and make our own membership fully aware of the political importance of the struggle for women's liberation.

5. Systematic education about the history of women's oppression and struggles, and the theoretical and political questions involved, should be organized within the sections of the Fourth International. This education should not be limited to special schools from time to time but must become part of the daily life of the organization. It must be part of the basic political education of each member as they acquire and deepen their understanding of the fundamental positions of revolutionary Marxism.

We have no illusions that sections can be islands of the future socialist society floating in a capitalist morass, or that individual comrades can fully escape the education and conditioning absorbed from the everyday effort to survive in class society. Sexist attitudes can and do sometimes find expression within the ranks of the Fourth International. But it is a condition of membership in the Fourth International that the conduct of comrades and sections be in harmony with the principles on which we stand. We educate the members of the Fourth International to a full understanding of the character of women's oppression and the pernicious ways in which it is expressed. We strive to create an organization in which language, jokes, personal violence, and other acts expressing chauvinist bigotry toward women are not tolerated, any more than acts and expressions of racist bigotry would be allowed to pass unchallenged.

6. Women members of our organizations face special problems, both material and psychological, stemming from their oppression in class society. They often face the same time-consuming domestic responsibilities as other women, especially if they have children. They are marked by the same lack of self-confidence, timidity, and fear of leadership that all women are educated from birth to consider as "natural." These obstacles to the recruitment, integration, and leadership development of women comrades must be discussed and consciously dealt with within the party.

As on all other questions, the leadership has the responsibility to take the lead:

Conscious attention must be given to the education, political development, and leadership training of women comrades. This should be a constant concern of all leadership bodies at all levels of the sections and the international. Consideration should be given to assuring that women are encouraged and, more importantly, helped to take on assignments that challenge them to develop their full capacities—teaching classes, writing articles, giving political reports, being public spokespersons and candidates for the organization, leading areas of work. Only by taking such deliberate and conscious measures can we maximize the development of our women cadre and assure that when they are elected to leadership bodies at all levels, this reflects a genuine expansion of a self-confident and strong political leadership cadre, not an artificial measure that can prove destructive to both individual comrades and the organization as a whole.

Within such a general framework of conscious leadership development, we strive to maximize the number of women in the central leadership bodies of our sections and sympathizing organizations and international.

This process will be facilitated by the fact that a growing number of comrades will be in the vanguard of women fighting their way into nontraditional jobs as part of the industrial working class. The self-confidence they gain from being part of the most powerful and organized sectors of the proletariat, the respect they earn from both male and female workers, and the experience they acquire as leaders of our class, are a crucial part of transforming the consciousness of our organization and developing party leaders who are women.

For women comrades especially the difficulties created by the gross inadequacy of state-funded child-care facilities are often a barrier to their full participation in meetings and other activities. As our sections grow and become more working class in composition, we will be recruiting more comrades who have children.

In our public activities and through our intervention in the mass movement, we strive to make broader social forces conscious of the need for organized child care. We try to win the labor movement to support and put high priority on the fight for socially organized and funded child-care services. We demand that mass workers organizations such as trade unions organize meeting times to facilitate the participation of women members, and utilize their resources to provide child-care facilities.

Internally our comrades must be constantly aware of the extra burdens and obstacles that stem from social and economic inequality generated by capitalism, especially for women and comrades of oppressed nationalities. We make allowances for this. In this perspective the leadership has the obligation to work with comrades who have family responsibilities to try to find collective solutions that will enable them to minimize the obstacles to their political activity. For example, when a comrade with children is asked to take on a full-time assignment, the leadership has the responsibility to discuss and try to resolve the special needs, financial or otherwise.

At the same time, we recognize that there are limits to what the party can do. The party itself cannot assume the material obligation to eliminate the economic and social inequalities among comrades created by class society. We cannot assure the social services capitalism does not provide. The party does not have a generalized obligation to provide child care in order to equalize the personal situations of all comrades, nor can child-care duties be imposed on any comrade.

Such an approach would change the very purpose and character of the party as a political organization. What binds us together is our common determination to destroy the system that perpetuates inequality, our agreement on the program to accomplish that aim, and our loyalty to the party based on that program.

The process of educating our own members will take place along with, and be facilitated by, the growing involvement of our sections in the struggle for women's liberation. The impact of this struggle on the consciousness and attitudes of all comrades has already been profound. The transformation of the women cadre of the international, reflecting our involvement in the struggle for women's liberation, is a development of historic dimensions. The growing self-confidence, political maturity, and leadership capacities of the women comrades of the Fourth International constitute a significant expansion of the effective forces of revolutionary leadership on a world scale.

The new rise of women's struggles internationally and the emergence of a strong women's liberation movement prior to revolutionary struggles for power is a development of prime importance to the world party of socialist revolution. It increases the political power of the working class and the likelihood that the international revolution will be successful in carrying through to the end its task of socialist reconstruction. The rise of the women's liberation movement is an additional guarantee against the bureaucratic degeneration of future revolutions.

The struggle to liberate women from the bondage in which class society has placed them is a struggle to free all human relationships from the shackles of economic compulsion and to propel humanity along the road to a higher social order.

NOVEMBER 1979

RESOLUTION ON INTERNAL WOMEN'S CAUCUSES

This resolution was submitted by the United Secretariat. The vote of delegates and fraternal observers was: 63 for, 36.5 against, 3 abstentions, 10.5 not voting.

In recent years a number of sections of the Fourth International have adopted resolutions permitting the organization of women's caucuses—that is, internal meetings open to women comrades only.

While we support and fight for the right of women to form such caucuses in non-Leninist organizations, we are opposed to such groups within the revolutionary party.

The emergence of women's caucuses in some sections has reflected very real political problems and leadership defaults.

There has been insensitivity to the depth of the special problems women comrades face, failure to understand the political importance of the women's liberation movement and its place in the class struggle, slowness in responding to the rise of the feminist movement, or reluctance to assign comrades to women's liberation work and integrate it into all arenas of our political activity. Because of these errors we have unnecessarily lost valuable cadres and political opportunities. This kind of situation has frequently led to an explosion of resentment by comrades, especially women, who recognize that sexist attitudes often underlie these errors and make them more difficult to correct.

In an effort to change this kind of situation, women comrades in a number of sections have demanded the right to meet together in caucuses, from which all male comrades are excluded, to discuss the internal situation in the party.

Our support for the right of women to caucus in organizations in the mass movement flows from the fact that other organizations are not based on a revolutionary Marxist program that represents the historical interests of women and the working class. Their leaderships are not democratically elected to defend such a program. There is a contradiction, for example, between the interests of the trade-union bureaucracy and the needs of the union membership and of women. In that situation the right to organize women's caucuses becomes a question of elementary democracy and part of the struggle to put the union on a class-struggle political course.

But the revolutionary Marxist party can accomplish the historic tasks it has set itself only if it is capable of uniting in its ranks and leadership the most conscious and combative representatives of the working class and especially its most oppressed and exploited layers. To do this it must overcome the deep divisions fostered by capitalism and forge a cadre that has profound confidence in its common commitment and understanding of the tasks. This is concretized in the program of the revolutionary Marxist party, which synthesizes the experiences, demands, and interrelation between the struggles of all the exploited and oppressed and integrates them in a strategic line of march toward the proletarian revolution.

From this program we derive our organizational norms. Just as we have only one program, we have only one class of membership. Every comrade, male or female, Black or white, worker or petty bourgeois, young or old, literate or illiterate, has the same rights when it comes to determining the party's program and activity, the same responsibilities for implementing those decisions. The party's political program, line of intervention, and internal functioning must be democratically discussed and decided with all members participating. All internal fractions, commissions, tendencies, or other formations must be organized democratically—i.e., open to all members assigned to a particular area of work or all members who agree on the platform of a tendency, regardless of sex, race, age, language, class origin, or whatever.

In a revolutionary Marxist party, whatever its shortcomings and weaknesses may be, there is no inherent contradiction between program, leadership, and ranks. Thus the organization of women-only caucuses cuts across the internal democracy of the party and the construction of the kind of organization we need to realize our working-class program.

Since they are usually established for the express purpose of discussing internal problems *only*, women's caucuses are incapable of charting a course to resolve internal contradictions. That can only be done by charting a correct course of intervention in the mass movement to build the party. In the process the membership is educated and transformed.

Repeated experiences have shown—in practice as well as in theory—that the formation of women's caucuses does not help to resolve the problems that led to their formation. Rather they create centrifugal dynamics, fostering the impression that the party is a federation of conflicting interest groups each one fighting for its own program and priorities rather than an organization united on the basis of a common program and assessment of tasks. Often the caucuses reinforce the attitude that it is only the women comrades who are responsible for resolving the problems. They turn the women in on themselves in a destructive way. They deepen the frustration and political disorientation of both male and female comrades, and often hasten rather than prevent the departure of women from the organization.

Because they are not based on internal democracy caucuses also undermine our centralism in action. They stand in contradiction to our program and our democratic centralist organizational norms.

Strong pressure to organize such caucuses is a danger sign that the *leadership* has failed to meet the political challenge of educating the party on all aspects of the struggle for women's liberation and its place in the work of the party. The problems cannot be resolved by condemning the women comrades who are seeking a solution. The response must be fundamentally political, not organizational, and the leadership must take the responsibility for correcting errors, educating and leading.

The problems that exist can be resolved only through a full political discussion leading to (a) the implementation of consistent work on women's liberation, integrated into all areas of activity; and (b) conscious measures of cadre development which can integrate women comrades and overcome sexist habits and attitudes.

NOVEMBER 1979

SOCIAL WEIGHT AND REVOLUTIONARY STRATEGY FOR THE TRANSFORMATION OF THE LABOR MOVEMENT

Excerpt from 'A new stage of revolutionary working-class politics'
Report adopted by SWP National Committee, April 29, 1979

by Jack Barnes

Social weight

We also have to look more closely at the social weight of various political struggles today. This has a great deal to do with how we set our priorities, and how we allocate our resources.

We define the political importance of all issues by the social weight of the section of the population affected by it. By this, we don't mean the size of some layer of the population. We are not talking simply about numbers. For example, working farmers, as producers of vital food and fiber commodities, have greater social weight than college students. This is true even though there are more college students than farmers.

We're also not talking primarily about conjunctures, about the ups and downs in how much public attention is focused on an issue at any particular time. Social weight cannot be gauged by the relative size of demonstrations around various issues at any given time.

By social weight, we are gauging *the relationship to the working class* of various layers of the population and of the issues that affect them. We're talking about social power and potential political clout. As revolutionists we begin from the understanding that the most powerful, the decisive social force is the working class, which must govern, and that the industrial workers are its most powerful component.

This criterion of social weight holds even in a country where the working class is a minority of the population. What we're interested in is the relationship of the struggles of social layers, nationalities, and oppressed groups to the working class. How these struggles relate to all the things the working class as a whole must fight for and conquer on its way to being able to govern. How they help advance the transformation of the unions.

This class framework provides a way to determine the sections of the American population with the greatest social weight: Blacks, Chicanos, Puerto Ricans, women, farmers, the youth. These sections of the population play a central role in the economic, social, and political structure of capitalism. Their struggles and demands pose a profound challenge to capitalist rule.

Take the fight against racism, for example. The fight for Black and Chicano rights especially. This is central not only because of the size and history of the nonwhite populations. It is also crucial because of the percentage of Blacks and Chicanos in the working class, the proletarian composition of these oppressed nationality populations, and the resulting stake of the working class, as a class, in all the questions confronting Blacks and Chicanos.

Women make up more than half the working class and around 40 percent of the labor force. More than 50 percent of all women between sixteen and fifty-five are in the work force today, and more are entering.

The superexploitation of these layers drags down the wages and job conditions of all workers and is a source of enormous profits for the capitalists. The employers introduce racist and sexist prejudices into the working class in order to keep the oppressed and exploited weak and divided; this becomes especially crucial to the employers at times of rising class combativity. In addition, the oppression of women is vital to the family, which is an indispensable social and economic unit in capitalist society.

It's for these reasons that the demands raised by the oppressed nationalities and women are in both the immediate and the historic interests of the entire working class. The fight around these demands plays a central role in the mobilization and transformation of the labor movement. They advance the unity and self-confidence of our class and point toward the fight for a workers' government to restructure all social relations and wipe out all oppression and exploitation.

All political struggles are aspects of the class struggle. But that is merely the beginning of wisdom. We have to recognize that some issues are central to the line of march of our class, while others are peripheral. Some of the central issues are imperialist war, unemployment, inflation, social breakdowns, atomic radiation, race and sex discrimination, police brutality, restrictions on democratic rights.

Without fighting around these issues, the working class cannot prepare itself to govern, cannot marshal the allies it needs to fight for power, and—more and more—cannot even guarantee its physical survival.

How did we determine that the death penalty is a central political issue, for example? After all, it only directly affects several hundred people right now. But we say that capital punishment is a weighty question, nonetheless, because it has to do with class exploitation and oppression. It's not the capitalists who suffer from the death penalty in the United States today. It's the working class, and within the working class it's the oppressed nationalities who suffer most. The death penalty is a weapon of terror wielded by the ruling class and its courts against the working class, especially the most oppressed sectors, in order to keep them cowed. That's what makes it an important question, not just our sense of moral outrage that this brutal ruling class claims the right to murder human beings.

Social weight is a very important guide to us in deciding how to use our resources most efficiently. What our comrades should be doing. Which organizations or coalitions we should be participating in, to what extent, and to what ends. It helps us determine which issues are more peripheral to the workers' march to power, and the practical conclusions we must draw from that judgment.

It helps us determine that the question of imperialist war is weightier than the death penalty, but that both are central issues for our class.

It tells us that the *Weber* affirmative-action fight[1] should be a central party campaign, while we choose to throw less resources into the just struggle around Indian fishing rights.

It tells us that the fights for ERA ratification, abortion rights, and child care have greater social weight than the struggle for legislation guaranteeing full civil and human rights for gays and lesbians.

It guides us in relating to issues such as the repeal of marijuana laws, the rights of the handicapped, and saving wilderness areas and endangered species. We support these demands, publicize them in the *Militant* when struggles around them arise, solidarize with them. But we do not allocate major forces to intervene in coalitions organized around them.

This relates to another of the litanies that sometimes crops up in our press or in leaflets. We will sometimes, without stopping to think about it, reel off this list of victims of capitalist oppression: "Blacks, Chicanos, women, gays." But this creates an inaccurate impression of our judgment on the social weight of these four groups. The social weight of gays is qualitatively less than that of Blacks, Chicanos, and women.

The social weight criteria also help us understand more fully our class approach to the fight for democratic rights.

Democratic rights are indivisible—that is, the denial or abuse of the rights of any section of the population is a threat to all democratic rights. Any denial of democratic rights is against the interests of the working class and must be fought by the labor movement.

While democratic rights are indivisible in this fundamental sense, however, they are not all politically equal in terms of strategic importance, in social weight. The democratic rights that are most crucial to the proletariat are freedom of speech, the right to assemble, the right to organize, freedom of the press, etc. Without rights such as these, the

---

1. Brian Weber, a white lab technician at Kaiser Aluminum in Gramercy, Louisiana, filed suit against the affirmative-action provisions of the USWA's 1974 contract with Kaiser charging "reverse discrimination." The Steelworkers, other major unions, and the AFL-CIO defended the affirmative-action provisions and, in June 1979, the U.S. Supreme Court rejected Weber's challenge.

working class cannot organize as a class economically or politically.

The other category of democratic rights most crucial to the working class includes those that directly affect the most proletarian sections of the population and those of its most decisive allies. The rights of Blacks and Chicanos, for example, from self-determination on down to every aspect of the fight against racism and discrimination. The rights of women. The rights of youth.

Finally, social weight helps us give a clearer definition, a class definition to a term that is sometimes misused—the term *radical*. That word doesn't communicate much unless it's given a class definition. Is a tactic radical if it's wild? Is an issue radical just because it's shocking to bourgeois morality and respectability? Was the brutal, capitalist Pol Pot regime radical? Fascists are radical, aren't they?

We, of course, mean something very precise when we use the word; we're giving it a class definition. Building opposition to the *Weber* suit is radical. Telling the truth about Newport News is radical.

The labor party is a very radical concept, although many petty-bourgeois "radicals" don't think so. It is a historic, radical break by our class from dependence on the Democratic and Republican parties, the parties of the capitalist exploiters.

No separate roads

We often used to say that the winning strategy in the antiwar movement was mass demonstrations. But that wasn't a strategy. That was a specific tactic that we often advocated, flowing from our overall strategy, which was a working-class strategy. We consistently fought for political demands and methods of struggle that would maximize the opportunities to draw in the working class, the unions, the GIs, Blacks, and Chicanos. That was our aim. It was the best way to defend the Vietnamese revolution and the best way to move forward the consciousness and mobilization of our class.

But properly understood, we do have a mass-action strategy—a strategy of mobilizing our class in action around a program that represents its historic interests. The shah of Iran was brought down by the mass action of the Iranian workers and their allies. Strikes, factory committees, soviets, insurrections, workers' militias—all these elements of the organization and mobilization of the workers and our allies outlined in the Transitional Program are forms of mass working-class action.

But we don't have a "mass demonstration" strategy, in the sense of a "march on Washington" strategy. Those are tactics.

We don't have a collection of separate isolated winning strategies for various social struggles. One for the Black struggle. One for the fight for women's rights. One for the antinuclear movement.

We have a strategy for the revolutionary transformation of the labor movement and for the use of that power to transform society. We have a strategy to mobilize our class and its allies to fight for a workers' government.

From *that* strategic framework, we can figure out what steps are necessary to advance all progressive struggles. How they can link up with the decisive social power needed to win. What tactics can advance the overall fight against oppression and capitalist misrule.

What do we mean when we say that a social protest movement is "independent"? First, we mean that it must be independent of the ruling class. We also mean that it should fight resolutely for its demands. It shouldn't subordinate its goals, or wait on other social forces, including the unions, to take up its banner before taking up the fight itself.

But these movements *cannot* be independent of the shifts in the relationship of class forces. They *cannot* be independent from the influence and pressures of the two main contending classes. And they *must not* be independent of a working-class strategy to move forward and to transform the labor movement. Otherwise they have no hope of securing any lasting victories, because that's where the power to transform society lies.

More and more, it's hard to make even small gains, or defend past gains, without applying this strategic understanding. That's what we mean in pointing out that there can be no separate strategies for these struggles.

This doesn't in any way mean that struggles that erupt outside the labor movement should wait, or that they are less important today than they were in the past. To the contrary.

With correct leadership and a conscious working-class strategy and program, these struggles can play a decisive role in advancing the transformation of American labor. They can help drive forward the process of getting the unions to think socially and act politically. They can help in the development of a class-struggle left wing necessary to get the bureaucracy off the backs of the working class, so that union power can be used on behalf of all the oppressed and exploited.

But they will be able to do so only to the extent a leadership that is proletarian both in composition and outlook comes forward. A leadership that is conscious of where it's going, what it's doing, and why it must link up with the power of American labor.

Every single social protest movement today badly needs a pamphlet like George Breitman's *How a Minority Can Change Society*.[2] Because they have the untapped potential to put forces into motion that will deeply affect the working class—the social power that can and must change society from top to bottom.

---

2. George Breitman, *How a Minority Can Change Society* (New York: Pathfinder Press, 1965, 1969).

In saying this, of course, we always recognize that while each of these struggles is an aspect of the class struggle, each has a special character, a different specific political function. It's not their job to directly forge a class-struggle left wing in the unions; they couldn't do that if they wanted to. That will be done by the most class-conscious workers as they run into the necessity to use union power to fight around all aspects of the rulers' offensive.

So our insistence that these movements have no *separate* winning strategy is not a prescription for abstention. It's the opposite—a guide to participation and intervention.

As the revolutionary socialist wing of the American labor movement, we participate in important social struggles to bring a working-class perspective, the only winning perspective, into the fight. We are socialist workers who want to bring the power of our class and our unions into the struggle around these issues. And we want to raise these vital questions in our unions as part of our strategic goal of transforming the unions into instruments of revolutionary social and political change.

AFFIRMATIVE ACTION GAINS FOR WOMEN IN INDUSTRY AND THE WAY FORWARD FOR THE WOMEN'S MOVEMENT

Excerpt from 'A new stage of revolutionary working-class politics'
Report adopted by SWP National Committee, April 29, 1979

by Jack Barnes

Women's movement in crisis

We face a similar crisis of leadership in the women's movement. And this crisis is not lessened by the existence of NOW as a national organization.

The political problem is evident when you read the *National NOW Times*. Last month, for example, an award was given by Philadelphia NOW to the first woman to become a police detective in that city. That's literally true. A cop! The *National NOW Times* also ran a several-column article, with photo, of a meeting organized by NOW to have a "dialogue" and seek "consensus" on the issue of birth control with antiabortion groups.

There is a crisis facing women in this country regarding abortion. The right to abortion—that is, economic, social, and political access—is being brutally cut back. This is not because workers are turning against abortion rights. A Gallup poll released just a few days ago showed there has been no decline whatsoever since 1975 in the percentage of people who support abortion rights. But the economic possibility of having an abortion, and the availability of facilities, have been sharply limited by federal and state legislation. This is one of the "take-backs" the ruling class has implemented since the offensive began in 1974–75.

It will take a social battle to reestablish this right in real life. The "one-sided class war" has come down especially hard on Black and Chicana women, on women of the other oppressed nationalities, and on all working women.

The fight for the Equal Rights Amendment is in crisis, too. The NOW leadership has reduced this struggle fundamentally to organizing political support for Democratic Party politicians, together with attempts to talk people out of taking their vacations in states that have not ratified the ERA.

We give the same answer to the crisis of NOW as we do to that of Black organizations such as the NAACP. There is no "independent strategy" for women that can win. There is no tricky tactic that can circumvent the crisis. There are correct tactics, tactics that can move the struggle ahead, but they must be timely expressions of a strategic vision that places the women's liberation movement in a class perspective. That's the only way to assemble the necessary social forces to win the abortion fight, or win the ERA.

Key to the road forward is the transformation, the revolution, that is taking place as women in the labor force push their way into industry. This transformation began as one of the repercussions of the gains of the Black struggle. When the Civil Rights Act was being debated in Congress in 1964, the southern senators tried to prevent its passage by outlawing discrimination in employment on the basis of sex as well as race. They figured that made Title VII, as that clause of the act is known, so ridiculous, even northern liberals would have to vote against it. But it was passed.

Affirmative-action drive

This provided a legal opening for the affirmative-action drive by women. It gave women a legal club to use to force their way not just into jobs, but into basic industry, with its higher wages and greater unionization. Thousands of suits were filed. One stride forward came with the 1974 consent decree in the basic steel industry which established plantwide seniority and set hiring goals for women and apprenticeship goals for women, Blacks, and Latinos. From 1975 to 1979, women made a big push into auto, mining, and steel.

Jobs in industry are key to women for several reasons. One is that secretaries, teachers, and social workers simply do not have the raw power that industrial workers have when it comes to winning women's rights or anything else.

But it's more than that. Opening the doors to basic industry has a powerful impact on the consciousness and self-confidence of women, and on the way that men view their female co-workers. Many deeply ingrained attitudes change rapidly. The interconnections between the workers' struggle against class exploitation and women's struggle for economic independence and full equality come to life. Sexist prejudices begin to break down.

The women's movement needs to make the same kind of shift that is necessary for the Black and Chicano movements. To win the ERA, abortion rights, and the other demands of women today will take a stronger, different kind of movement than a decade ago, with a different kind of leadership. But the forces exist to build such a movement.

Working women, and especially women in industry, have to lead this process, orienting the women's movement towards a strategic axis that can push the movement forward. This includes, of course, the fight against discrimination and harassment on the job. It's not sexual harassment only. The term is too narrow. The fight against sexual harassment is one aspect of the much broader fight of working women—the fight against the harassment of women as a sex, against discrimination, and for the right to get jobs, to hold them, and to have full rights on those jobs.

At the same time that working women need to become involved in the women's movement, they must also take their struggles into the unions, to win support for abortion rights, pregnancy benefits, the ERA, and other needs.

This is the direction the women's liberation movement must go. Not toward the antiabortion forces that support birth control. Not toward women cops or detectives.

This is what we have been raising and arguing in organizations like NOW for nearly two years, ever since we and women we were allied with in NOW drew up the "Defending Women's Rights" resolution in 1977.

What faces the women's movement is a political question and a class question, the same as with the Black movement. The leadership of the women's movement is petty-bourgeois. But the forces coming forward in struggle are working-class women. At the same time there is a growing radicalization among other layers of the working class, including male workers.

The fact that we now have many more comrades in industry allows us to alter the way we do our women's liberation work. Comrades in industry must play an increasing role in the various women's organizations. We need to take another look at what we do in NOW. Instead of shaping our work in the unions to work in NOW, we need to orient our proposals in NOW to meet the changing needs and potential of women in industry. We have to fight in NOW for involving the labor movement in the battle for women's rights.

Our work in the factories and the unions must become the axis of our women's liberation work. We need to pay close attention to the women's caucuses and committees in the unions and in the plants. We should even take a new look at various local units of the Coalition of Labor Union Women (CLUW). No organization of this type should be written off. Because the fighting women's organizations that are going to emerge from the struggles beginning today will not look like anything that exists right now.

The character of NOW as a large national organization gives it a special importance. Its links with the labor movement are also important.

There are two sides to the Smeal-Fraser alliance, for example. On the one hand, it represents an alliance between a section of the labor bureaucracy and the leadership of NOW in an attempt to subordinate the women's movement to the needs of the capitalist class, just as the unions are subordinated. This has political implications. Fraser tells Smeal that just electing Democratic Party candidates is insufficient; all progressive forces must work together to reform the Democratic Party.

But there is another side to this collaboration between NOW and a section of organized labor. It reflects pressure coming from below. It reflects the new consciousness that women have of themselves and their fellow male workers, and their search for powerful allies. From this point of view, the mutual interests of Smeal and Fraser provide an important opening.

Against the employers, foremen, politicians

The axis of women's fight is against the employers, their foremen, their courts, and their politicians—not against fellow workers. To the contrary, women should aggressively *appeal to* all the class-struggle-minded workers on the job, seeking support for women's rights. From our initial experience, we know there is usually a positive response when women fight along these lines. Women in and out of industry can see the attractive power of the labor movement and the potential for support from layers of young, militant workers.

This came through clearly at a District 31 conference of USWA. An older, Black, male worker got up at this conference and explained:

We have to support the women. The bosses are doing to them just what they did to us when we first came in the mill. They're trying to drive them out. Women still have to fight to establish their right to remain in industry.

This Black steelworker predicted that with the next major downturn, women will face a concerted drive to push them out of industry.

He was absolutely right.

This is one reason we should approach women's committees or caucuses in the unions differently today than Black or Chicano caucuses. We favor and sometimes help initiate women's committees or caucuses, while we don't initiate Black or Chicano caucuses for the reasons I outlined earlier. Of course, we know that working women, like Blacks and Chicanos, will help blaze the trail toward a class-struggle left wing in the unions. They will play a vanguard role in the transformation of the labor movement.

But we have to recognize the different positions of Blacks and women in industry today, the different stage women are at in getting into industry and staying there.

Women face greater obstacles because of their small numbers and their newness in industry. They have to fight the bosses, the foremen, and the whole setup just to prevent themselves from being driven out of the plants. Often the forms don't exist for women to work through these problems and figure out how to use their unions to defend their rights. Special women's committees, as in District 31 of the USWA and in many auto locals, can provide such a form.

Added to this are the special obstacles women face, because of the character of women's oppression in class society, in becoming self-confident leaders of their class and their unions in leading their male co-workers. This is a bigger problem for women than for Blacks, Chicanos, and other oppressed national minorities. It's another reason why women's committees can play a very positive role.

The importance of fighting 'Weber'

The fight by women to get into industry and hang on there also underscores the centrality of the affirmative-action question and the *Weber* case. The importance we have given this fight has been proven correct by one simple thing: the growing number of workers, including male workers and white workers, who are beginning to understand that affirmative action is a *class* question, a question that involves the effectiveness of their unions. The ability to explain this through the *Weber* case is made easier by the fact that the suit also challenges union collective bargaining rights around the issue of job discrimination and upgrading.

Today, Black, Chicano, and women workers as a group comprise a significant percentage of the membership of the major industrial unions. This makes it easier for other unionists to see why, in the interests of solidarity against the bosses' offensive, they must combat discrimination. This mounting pressure from below, in turn, has forced the majority of the labor officialdom to come out in formal opposition to *Weber*. It is responsible for the USWA bureaucracy's decision to fight the case in the courts and to call the recent civil rights conference.

This is an important new development, a promising new trend in the American labor movement.

Of course, it's just a beginning. There is still a big fight ahead to demand that the labor officialdom throw union power behind this struggle, which it has no intention of doing today. There is still a big job in educating workers, especially white workers and male workers, about their stake in the fight and mobilizing them into action around it.

But the opportunities to do this are greater than ever before. More and more workers are willing to listen and agree when opponents of discrimination explain that affirmative action is vitally and directly in the interests of the working class as a class. Affirmative action is not a charity to make up for the past. It's not—as some argue—a morally correct position but materially disadvantageous to males and whites.

Workers are better able today to grasp aspects of the political economy of discrimination—that discrimination does not mean an extra buck for some workers at the expense of women or of Blacks, Chicanos, or Puerto Ricans; instead, it drags the whole class down in terms of real wages and job conditions, and saps the collective ability to fight back against the bosses.

More and more workers are waking up to their class interests, which do not lie in seeking privileges for some. As this happens, they become more capable of seeing the difference between class struggle and class collaboration, between themselves and the union bureaucrats. It becomes clear that it *strengthens* the union to bring in more Blacks, Chicanos, Puerto Ricans, and, yes, women, to make sure that everyone gets the *same treatment*.

There are more and more openings for us to explain and move forward along this axis of struggle.

But we must add the point we made in the March 30, 1979, *Militant* editorial: The kinds of struggles that established the principle of affirmative action will not be sufficient to defend or extend it. More powerful forces and a more conscious leadership are going to be necessary for that.

The *Militant* editorial noted that the civil rights laws were won without the unions really entering the fray. The editorial continued: "This is a new period, in which the capitalist economy is wracked by crisis; in which the employers are driven to harsher and harsher antilabor attacks in order to defend their profits. This is a period of polarization of class forces.

"The only class that has an interest in defending affirmative action is the working class. And the fight to defend affirmative action must be taken right to the center of the only mass organizations of the working class—the unions."

WOMEN'S LIBERATION AND SOCIALISM

Women in Cuba: The Making of a Revolution Within the Revolution
VILMA ESPÍN, ASELA DE LOS SANTOS, YOLANDA FERRER

The integration of women in the ranks and leadership of the Cuban Revolution was intertwined with the proletarian course of the leadership of the revolution from the start. This is the story of that revolution and how it transformed the women and men who made it. $17. Also in Spanish, Farsi, and Greek.

Feminism and the Marxist Movement
MARY-ALICE WATERS

Since the founding of the modern revolutionary workers movement nearly 150 years ago, Marxists have championed the struggle for women's rights and explained the economic roots in class society of women's oppression. "The struggle for women's liberation," Waters writes, "was lifted out of the realm of the personal, the 'impossible dream,' and unbreakably linked to the progressive forces of our epoch"—the working-class struggle for power. $5. Also in Farsi.

Women's Liberation and the African Freedom Struggle
THOMAS SANKARA

"There is no true social revolution without the liberation of women," explains the leader of the 1983–87 revolution in the West African country of Burkina Faso. $5. Also in Spanish, French, and Farsi.

Capital
KARL MARX

The best book ever written on the oppression of women, their exploitation in modern society, and the road to emancipation. Three volumes, $18 each. Also in Spanish.

Woman's Evolution
From Matriarchal Clan to Patriarchal Family
EVELYN REED

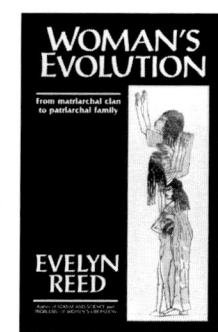

An expedition from prehistory to class society that reveals women's still largely unknown contributions to civilization. Pinpointing the historical factors that led to the subordination of women as a sex, Reed offers fresh insights on the struggle against their oppression and for the liberation of humanity. $25. Also in Farsi and Indonesian.

Marianas in Combat
Teté Puebla and the Mariana Grajales Women's Platoon in Cuba's Revolutionary War 1956–58
TETÉ PUEBLA

Brigadier General Teté Puebla, the highest ranking woman in Cuba's Revolutionary Armed Forces, joined the struggle to overthrow the US-backed dictatorship of Fulgencio Batista in 1956, when she was fifteen years old. This is her story—from clandestine action in the cities, to serving as an officer in the victorious Rebel Army's first all-women's unit. The fight to transform the social and economic status of women in Cuba remains inseparable from its socialist revolution. $10. Also in Spanish and Farsi.

Women and the Family
LEON TROTSKY

How the October 1917 Russian Revolution, the first victorious socialist revolution, opened the door to new possibilities in the fight for women's liberation. $10

The Emancipation of Women
V.I. LENIN

On women's equality. Including Clara Zetkin's interview with Lenin and a preface by N.K. Krupskaya. $7

WWW.PATHFINDERPRESS.COM

$12 $15 $20

Three books to be read as one . . .

about building a party that's working class in program, composition, and action. One that recognizes, in word and deed, the most revolutionary fact of our time . . .

. . . that working people have the power to create a different world as we act together to defend our own class interests—not those of the privileged classes who exploit our labor, not of those who fear us as "deplorables," or just plain "trash."

As we advance along a revolutionary course toward workers power, we will transform ourselves and awaken to our own worth. Also in Spanish and French.

The Turn to Industry and
Tribunes of the People and the Trade Unions
$20

Either book plus *Malcolm X, Black Liberation, and the Road to Workers Power*
$25

Special Offer! All three $30

Workers and the US rulers' deepening political crisis

Three books for today's spreading and deepening debate among working people looking for a way forward in face of capitalism's global economic and social calamity and wars.

Are They Rich Because They're Smart?
Class, privilege, and learning under capitalism
JACK BARNES

Also in Spanish, French, Farsi, and Arabic.
$10.

The Clintons' Anti-Working-Class Record
Why Washington fears working people
JACK BARNES

Also in Spanish, French, Farsi, and Greek.
$10.

Is Socialist Revolution in the US Possible?
A necessary debate among working people
MARY-ALICE WATERS

Also in Spanish, French, and Farsi.
$7.

RELATED READINGS

The Transitional Program for Socialist Revolution
LEON TROTSKY

The Socialist Workers Party program, drafted by Trotsky in 1938, still guides the SWP and communists the world over. The party "uncompromisingly gives battle to all political groupings tied to the apron strings of the bourgeoisie. Its task—the abolition of capitalism's domination. Its aim—socialism. Its method—the proletarian revolution."

Also in Farsi.
$17.

Capitalism's World Disorder
Working-class politics at the millennium
JACK BARNES

The social devastation and financial crises, the coarsening of politics, the cop brutality and acts of imperialist aggression accelerating around us—all are products not of something gone wrong with capitalism but of its lawful workings. Yet the future can be changed by the united struggle and selfless action of working people conscious of their power to transform the world.

Also in Spanish and French.
$20.

WWW.PATHFINDERPRESS.COM

EXPAND YOUR REVOLUTIONARY LIBRARY

Labor, Nature, and the Evolution of Humanity
The Long View of History
FREDERICK ENGELS, KARL MARX, GEORGE NOVACK, MARY-ALICE WATERS

Why is it important to know that social labor, transforming nature, has been the motor force of humanity's evolution for millions of years? Because without that knowledge, working people are unable to see beyond the capitalist epoch, beyond the class exploitation that warps all human relations, ideas, and values. The dictatorship of capital had a beginning . . . and it will have an end. But only the revolutionary conquest of state power by the working class can open the door to a world free of capitalism's dog-eat-dog social reality. A world built on human solidarity. A socialist world. $12. Also in Spanish and French.

Lenin's Final Fight
Speeches and Writings, 1922–23
V.I. LENIN

In 1922 and 1923, V.I. Lenin, central leader of the world's first socialist revolution, waged what was to be his last political battle—one that was lost following his death. At stake was whether that revolution, and the international communist movement it led, would remain on the revolutionary proletarian course that brought workers and peasants to power in October 1917. $17. Also in Spanish, Farsi, and Greek.

50 Years of Covert Operations in the US
Washington's Political Police and the American Working Class
LARRY SEIGLE, FARRELL DOBBS, STEVE CLARK

How class-conscious workers have fought against the drive to build the "national security" state essential to maintaining capitalist rule. $10. Also in Spanish and Farsi.

W.E.B. Du Bois Speaks, 1920–1963
Speeches and Addresses

A comprehensive collection of speeches by the Black rights advocate and scholar. 2nd of 2 vols. $20

By Any Means Necessary
MALCOLM X

"The imperialists know the only way you will voluntarily turn to the fox is to show you a wolf." In eleven speeches and interviews, Malcolm X presents a revolutionary alternative to this reformist trap, taking up political alliances, women's rights, US intervention in the Congo and Vietnam, capitalism and socialism, and more. $15

Fighting Racism in World War II
FROM THE PAGES OF THE *MILITANT*

An account of struggles against racist discrimination in US war industries, the armed forces, and society as a whole from 1939 to 1945, taken from the pages of the socialist newsweekly, the *Militant*. These struggles helped lay the basis for the proletarian-based civil rights movement that followed. $20

Malcolm X Talks to Young People

"The young generation of whites, Blacks, browns, whatever else—you're living at a time of revolution," said Malcolm in 1964. "And I for one will join with anyone, I don't care what color you are, as long as you want to change this miserable condition that exists on this earth." Four talks and an interview in the last months of Malcolm's life. $12. Also in Spanish, French, Farsi, and Greek.

Cuba and the Coming American Revolution
JACK BARNES

This is a book about the struggles of working people in the imperialist heartland, the youth attracted to them, and the example set by the Cuban people that revolution is not only necessary—it can be made. It is about the class struggle in the US, where the revolutionary capacities of workers and farmers are today as utterly discounted by the ruling powers as were those of the Cuban toilers. And just as wrongly. $10. Also in Spanish, French, and Farsi.

Red Zone
Cuba and the Battle against Ebola in West Africa
ENRIQUE UBIETA GÓMEZ

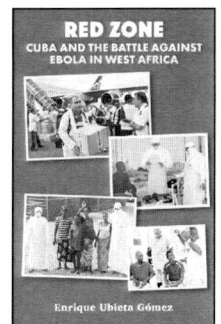

When three African countries were hit in 2014–15 by the Ebola epidemic, Cuba's revolutionary government sent what no other country even pretended to provide: more than 250 volunteer doctors, nurses, and other medical workers. This firsthand account of their actions shows the kind of men and women only a socialist revolution can produce. $17. Also in Spanish and French.

The History of the Russian Revolution
LEON TROTSKY

How, under Lenin's leadership, the Bolshevik Party led millions of workers and farmers to overthrow the state power of the landlords and capitalists in 1917 and bring to power a government that advanced their class interests at home and worldwide. Unabridged, 3 vols. in one. Written by one of the central leaders of that socialist revolution. $30. Also in French and Russian.

Maurice Bishop Speaks
The Grenada Revolution and Its Overthrow, 1979–83

The triumph of the 1979 revolution in the Caribbean island of Grenada under the leadership of Maurice Bishop gave hope to millions throughout the Americas. Invaluable lessons from the workers and farmers government destroyed by a Stalinist-led counterrevolution in 1983. $20

Democracy and Revolution
GEORGE NOVACK

The limitations and advances of various forms of democracy in class society, from its roots in ancient Greece through its rise and decline under capitalism. Discusses the emergence of Bonapartism, military dictatorship, and fascism, and how democracy will be advanced under a workers and farmers regime. $17

To See the Dawn
Baku, 1920—First Congress of the Peoples of the East

How can peasants and workers in the colonial world achieve freedom from imperialist exploitation? By what means can working people overcome divisions incited by their national ruling classes and act together for their common class interests? These questions were addressed by 2,000 delegates to the 1920 Congress of the Peoples of the East. $17

Cosmetics, Fashions, and the Exploitation of Women
JOSEPH HANSEN, EVELYN REED, MARY-ALICE WATERS

How big business reinforces women's second-class status and uses it to rake in profits. Where does women's oppression come from? How has the entry of millions of women into the workforce strengthened the battle for emancipation, still to be won? $12. Also in Spanish, Farsi, and Greek.

Lenin's Struggle for a Revolutionary International
Documents, 1907–1916; The Preparatory Years

The debate among revolutionary working-class leaders, including V.I. Lenin and Leon Trotsky, on a socialist response to World War I. $30

America's Revolutionary Heritage
Marxist Essays
GEORGE NOVACK

A materialist explanation of the American Revolution, Civil War and Radical Reconstruction, genocide against the Indians, rise of American imperialism, first wave of the fight for women's rights, and more. $23

WWW.PATHFINDERPRESS.COM

Labor's Giant Step
The First Twenty Years of the CIO: 1936–55
ART PREIS

The story of the explosive labor struggles and political battles in the 1930s that built the industrial unions. And how those unions became the vanguard of a mass social movement that began transforming US society. $27

Teamster Rebellion
FARRELL DOBBS

The 1934 strikes that won union recognition for truckers and warehouse workers in Minneapolis and helped pave the way for the working-class social movement that built the industrial unions. The first of four volumes by a central leader of these battles. $16. Also in Spanish, French, Farsi, and Greek.

The Jewish Question
A Marxist Interpretation
ABRAM LEON

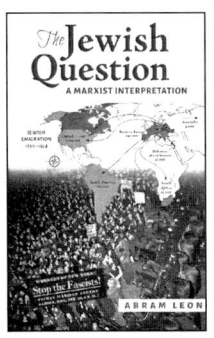

Why is Jew-hatred still raising its ugly head? What are its class roots—from antiquity through feudalism, to capitalism's rise and current crises? Why is there no solution under capitalism? The author, Abram Leon, was killed in the Nazi gas chambers. Revised translation, new introduction, and 40 pages of illustrations and maps. $17. Also in Spanish and French.

"It's the Poor Who Face the Savagery of the US 'Justice' System"
The Cuban Five Talk about Their Lives within the US Working Class

How US cops, courts, and prisons work as "an enormous machine for grinding people up." Five Cuban revolutionaries framed up and held in US jails for 16 years explain the human devastation of capitalist "justice"—and how socialist Cuba is different. $10. Also in Spanish, Farsi, and Greek.

U.S. Imperialism Has Lost the Cold War
JACK BARNES

The collapse of regimes across Eastern Europe and the USSR claiming to be communist did not mean workers and farmers there had been crushed. In today's sharpening capitalist conflicts and wars, these toilers are joining working people the world over in the class struggle against exploitation. In *New International* no. 11. $14. Also in Spanish, French, Farsi, and Greek.

The Revolution Betrayed
What Is the Soviet Union and Where Is It Going?
LEON TROTSKY

In 1917 workers and peasants of Russia were the motor force for one of the deepest revolutions in history. Yet within ten years a political counterrevolution by a privileged social layer, whose chief spokesperson was Joseph Stalin, was being consolidated. The classic study of the Soviet workers state and its degeneration. $17. Also in Spanish, Farsi, and Greek.

The Fight against Fascism in the USA
Forty Years of Struggle Described by Participants
JAMES P. CANNON AND OTHERS

In 1939 some 50,000 people in New York City responded to a call by the Socialist Workers Party to answer a pro-Nazi rally of 20,000. "The question of how to fight fascism was answered in thunderous tones by the magnificent demonstration which raised the cry: Workers Defense Guards to crush the fascist danger!" $5

We Are Heirs of the World's Revolutions
Speeches from the Burkina Faso Revolution, 1983–87
THOMAS SANKARA

How peasants and workers in this West African country established a popular revolutionary government and began to fight hunger, illiteracy, and economic backwardness imposed by imperialist domination. They set an example not only for workers and small farmers in Africa, but their class brothers and sisters the world over. $10. Also in Spanish, French, and Farsi.